Praise for *Ancient Sounds for a New Age* and Diáne Mandle

"Diane Mandle is the preeminent voice in the field of Tibetan bowl sound healing. Her book, Ancient Sounds for the New Age, offers a platform of deep understanding on which a practical skill set can be easily built upon. This is what the emerging field of sound healing has been waiting for. There is no doubt that it will soon be recognized as the go-to resource for serious vibrational practitioners.

As a long-time scholar and as a practitioner of vibrational healing I wholeheartedly recommend this book."

RICHARD RUDIS, KARMA SONAM DORJE

"When I first listened to Diáne Mandle play a Tibetan bowl I was literally out of this world, or, to say it better still, "above the world." I asked her to be a presenter at Rancho La Puerta so that guests could enjoy this as much as I have. The sound is eternal—and reminds you of eternity. Even in the most painful and stressful moments, it cleans the cobwebs and frees your mind to know that this, too, shall pass. Her book is a wonderful gift to all those who will find peace through the bowls' healing song."

DEBORAH SZEKELY, CO-FOUNDER, RANCHO LA PUERTA, FOUNDER, GOLDEN DOOR

"Diane has been a powerful presenter in several of our International Sound Healing retreats at Menla New York. She has a lengthy experience, understanding and spiritual relationship with the Himalayan Bowls. We are so grateful to have her share with us all the highest knowledge on these ambassadors of Peace in this new book. Dhanyavad."

PHILIPPE GARNIER, FOUNDER AND CO-DIRECTOR OF THE SAGE ACADEMY OF SOUND ENERGY IN NEW YORK AND THE ACADEMIE DE SONOTHÉRAPIE IN FRANCE.

"Diáne has a unique capacity of helping patients enhance their sense of well being and quality of life, especially in the midst of going through significant medical challenges including advanced cancer. Diáne does her healing work with great compassion, wisdom, devotion, love and deep care for those she is supporting. I can't wait for her new book to become available to anyone who wants to increase their knowledge of the power of Tibetan bowls sound to enhance healing, inner peace and sense of well being."

DANIEL VICARIO, M.D., ABIHM, MEDICAL ONCOLOGY AND INTEGRATIVE ONCOLOGY MEDICAL DIRECTOR AND DIRECTOR, INTEGRATIVE ONCOLOGY, SAN DIEGO CANCER RESEARCH INSTITUTE. 501(c)(3), INTEGRATIVE ONCOLOGY, MIND BODY MEDICAL GROUP, CHOPRA CENTER FOR WELLBEING

Ancient Sounds for a New Age

AN INTRODUCTION TO HIMALAYAN
SACRED SOUND INSTRUMENTS

ANCIENT SOUNDS FOR A NEW AGE

AN INTRODUCTION TO HIMALAYAN SACRED SOUND INSTRUMENTS

DIÁNE MANDLE

Illustrations by Cheryl di Ciantis and Richard Rudis

Life in Progress Publishing
ENCINITAS, CALIFORNIA

ISBN: 978-1-7334042-0-4 (paperback)
ISBN: 978-1-7334042-1-1 (ebook)

Library of Congress Control Number: 2019912867

Ancient Sounds for a New Age is published by: Life In Progress Publishing, 237 Cereus St., Encinitas, California USA

For information please direct emails to:
soundenergyhealing@gmail.com

Cover design, book layout and typography: Teri Rider & Associates
Illustrations: Cheryl di Ciantis, Richard Rudis

Printed in the United States of America

Please Note:
Though the author of this book is a certified Tibetan bowl healer, the information in this book is intended only as a guide to some of the processes of sound healing. The approaches, techniques, and suggestions described herein are meant to supplement, and not to be a substitute for, professional medical care or treatment. They should not be used to treat a serious ailment without prior consultation with a qualified health care practitioner. No advice given here should be taken in place of professional medical advice.

Dedication

To the community of Tibetans who have created and shared with us these amazing instruments of compassion and healing.

To my students and clients, who have always been my greatest teachers.

To Richard Rudis, for endless hours of love and support as I continually reinvented this book.

To my children, Isaiah and Stefan, who have helped me understand unconditional love.

To my mother whose support helped make this book possible.

Servant and master am I; servant of those dead, and master of those living. Through me spirits immortal speak the message that makes the world weep, and laugh, and wonder, and worship.

I tell the story of love, the story of hate, the story that saves and the story that damns. I am the incense upon which prayers float to Heaven. I am the smoke that palls over the field of battle where men lie dying with me on their lips.

I am close to the marriage altar, and when the graves open I stand nearby. I call the wanderer home, I rescue the soul form the depths, I open the lips of lovers, and through me the dead whisper to the living.

One I serve as I serve all; and the king I make my slave as easily as I subject his slave. I speak through the birds of the air, the insects of the field, the crash of waters on rock-ribbed shores, the sighing of wind in the trees, and I am even heard by the soul that knows me in the clatter of wheels on city streets.

I know no brother, yet all men are my brothers; I am the father of the best that is in them, and they are fathers of the best that is in me; I am of them and they are of me. For I am the instrument of God. I AM MUSIC.

AUTHOR UNKNOWN

Contents

Foreword by Richard Rudis

The year was 1998, and my dear friend remained motionless after a vibrational sojourn with Tibetan bowls as her guide. It was the usual period of consciousness and body rejoining that occurs after a session. I was unconcerned, knowing from the first that she was prepared for such a journey. As I watched the process of integration naturally progress, I realized just how ready she was for this deep, fundamental healing. After all, she was already an accomplished energetic healer (a polarity practitioner) and an effective life coach.

Some participants in such a healing return from the nurturing experience dazed, and after some grounding techniques, wander off to process in their own time. My friend arose into the present fully aware and with just one question: "I had a visitation—it was Buddha floating over me, blessing me, healing me, guiding me. The only strange thing is that he was entirely blue. Does that have meaning?"

I was astonished. Not by the visitation—many bodhisattvas participate on energetic levels (that is their job)—but by the sheer power of the experience and her innocence. Having no previous knowledge of a blue Buddha, she questioned: Why blue? She had just stood in the radiance of the Lapis Lazuli Buddha, the Medicine Buddha, venerated for his healing powers, the principle guide of healers. I now know that this was a pivotal moment, a prognostication of things to come.

This was Diáne Mandle's introduction to sacred sound healing. Over the years she has grown in awareness and ability, merging her healing gifts to create an effective, innovative, and unique healing modality. She has had remarkable successes, yet continues to work hard to gain insights and expand her healing techniques into new venues of effectiveness, striving to make this powerful healing practice more accessible. People praise her concert performances and recordings, and I am certain they will laud this book as well.

I believe Diáne is guided by the Medicine Buddha and I am honored to be a part of the process.

Ancient Sounds for a New Age is a wonderful workbook and a valuable point of departure into the realm of vibrational healing. There is much to learn and there are no complete, definitive works yet available. Through her own personal alchemy, however, Diáne has managed to create a manual that the reader can use with complete confidence. I can wholeheartedly recommend the techniques and observations found within these pages.

You are embarking on a remarkable journey with deep ramifications, the details of which can only be guessed at. I congratulate both author and reader on their partnership in physical, mental, and spiritual awakening.

Namaste,
Richard Rudis (Sonam Dorje)

Introduction

In the spring of 1998 I was staffing a booth at a weekend Whole Health Expo in Northampton, Massachusetts. I was a certified polarity practitioner and life coach, and I was at the expo to introduce attendees to my services. The booth next to mine contained an intriguing array of beautiful Himalayan bowls and other instruments. It was the first time I had seen such things, and I got to chatting with Richard, the owner of the booth. We talked a great deal that weekend, and we were interested in each other's work, so we agreed to trade sessions after the show.

My first session with the bowls blew my mind. The experience isn't one I can fully describe in words but I will try. I found myself in an amazing, transcendent state of no body—and my mind stopped thinking as well. It was a wonderful kind of soaring emptiness, boundlessness, limitlessness. Perhaps you have had the experience of traveling, waking up in the morning in a new place, and at first having no idea where in the world you are. There is a moment before you orient yourself and recall who you are and what you're doing and why you are in this new place, a brief emptiness before you reassume your identity as you have come to know yourself. It was like that, only it went on for an extended period of time. I was being introduced to my *diamond self,* the true essence of my being.

Though my mind was very free, I was acutely aware of one thing during that first session: a vivid and persistent image of a big blue Buddha floating above me and looking down, seeming somehow to be presiding over my session. When the session was over, I tried to convey to Richard what an amazing experience I had just had. I described it as best I could, including the blue Buddha.

"The Buddha was blue," I said. "I think he might have been sick or something."

Richard shook his head. "No," he said. "The blue Buddha is actually the traditional Medicine Buddha." Later, I learned that this Buddha is sometimes called the Supreme Healer, and I decided that he had been a reflection of something within myself. But right then as I was coming out of the session, the blue Buddha's message to me was clear:

This. I need to learn how to do this. *This is my calling!*

As it turned out, the man selling Himalayan bowls was Richard Rudis, an American practitioner and scholar of Vajrayana Buddhism, a sound pioneer and gong master who had been teaching people how to use the sacred instruments since 1988. He became my first sound healing teacher. I could not have asked for a better introduction to a practice that I have since made my own, and I embarked on a certification course, becoming the first graduate of Richard's sacred sound workshop series.

After a couple of years I moved from the East Coast to California to set up a practice combining my skills in polarity healing and coaching with the transformational, energy-shifting power of the sacred instruments. I had spent many, many hours learning how to play them and becoming familiar with the subtleties and nuances of the sounds they produced, as well as with which types of configurations and movements produced which kinds of energy shifts.

At first, I was one of the few people on the West Coast to use Himalayan bowls and other traditional instruments. Everyone was intrigued, and I delighted in introducing people to these amazing tools through healing sessions and educational concerts. Then, a few years later, suddenly everyone seemed to be interested in the bowls. Cheap versions started showing up in all kinds of stores, and people began advertising workshops that claimed to teach you everything you needed to know to start your own sound healing practice, complete with a certificate proclaiming your expertise—in a *weekend*. Sound healing had become a fad.

I was beyond uncomfortable with this new development—I was distressed! For years I had seen firsthand how powerfully the instruments could affect just about every dimension of human health, and I was genuinely alarmed to think that someone with just a few hours' experience could establish a healing practice. I didn't doubt the sincere desire on the part of the students to use the instruments to help people, but I knew that all the good intentions in the world could not prevent downright harmful energy shifts from happening. In discussing this with Richard one day, I realized, *I need to start a school.* I urgently felt the need to establish a standard of practice for the field and a set of criteria for excellence in the skills necessary to ensure the personal safety of sound healing clients. I started the Tibetan Bowl Sound Healing School in 2008 with Richard, who helped develop curriculum and co-taught the advanced workshops.

What's Inside This Book?

This book is the direct result of my experience teaching hundreds of people over the intervening years. My aim for it is to offer beginners an introduction to and overview of sound healing with Himalayan instruments. I want to give you a clear idea of what you will need to learn and practice should you decide to enter the field, and I hope to inspire you to commit to patiently undertaking the serious study that is required. I also want to share my unique perspective with more experienced practitioners, as I have combined techniques from other fields that have proven very effective for my clients and describe these in the book.

The book is organized in four parts. The first, Fundamentals of Sound Healing, offers an orientation to the work, including frameworks for illness and healing, the role of intention and affirmation, and how a sound healing session generally flows.

Next, in Part II, The Sound Healing Family, you will learn about the sound healing instruments—the *tingshas,* the *ganta* and *dorje,* and the Himalayan bowls—and I will take you through some basic configurations for working with multiple instruments.

Part III, Sound Healing and the Chakras, takes us deeper with a breakdown of techniques and principles for working with the body's main energy centers, the *chakras.* Being aware of these centers and working with them, both directly and indirectly, gives further structure to a sound healing session and offers an effective way to create the energy shifts people need.

In Part IV, Working with Challenging Emotions, I offer brief orientations to working with anxiety and depression, dedicating one chapter to each. In your future practice with clients, you will find that both of these states come up a lot, so I want to preview the kinds of work you can do to shift that energy.

The last main section of the book, Part V, Enhancing Your Practice, concerns ways you can include other modalities in a sound healing session, and here I will share some that have worked well for me in my own practice. We will look at colors and toning, power language, and visualization. Remember: in learning to practice sound healing, we are aspiring to become more than *technicians* who can play the instruments—we are developing into *healers.*

Finally, at the back of the book in the appendices section, you will find thumbnail profiles of some sound healing pioneers, an interesting case study, some client testimonials, and further resources, including information about my school and some of the classes and products we offer.

How to Use This Book

You will get the most out of this book if, before practicing any of the techniques, you read Parts I and II through completely once and watch the companion DVD, also called *Ancient Sounds for a New Age,* available on YouTube: http://youtu.be/gSRqo8VMDuI. The video will give you a very good overall orientation to this healing modality—and you'll get to see and hear the instruments! Then, when you are ready to start practicing, you can turn this book into a personalized workbook. I suggest you read through it in bite-sized pieces, making notes on your experience as you go as well as charts to help you recall. That way, you will be able to quickly refer to particular areas of interest as you work with your practice partners.

Before you do any of this, though, I want to leave you with a couple of quick thoughts.

Practice Partners Versus Clients

Throughout this book you will find that I use "practice partner" and "client" interchangeably. This is done with the understanding that there is a continuum of learning, and that when you are in the beginning stages you will be working with friends, family, and acquaintances who are willing to support you while you put in the hundreds of hours it takes to build your skills. One day, though, assuming that you take to this work, you will have a professional practice of your own. Rest assured that everything you learn with your practice partners will apply to your future clients as well.

Practice with Healthy Partners

As I've said, this is a book mostly for beginners, and thus I want to be sure to caution you: *when you are just learning sound healing with these instruments, be sure you only work with people who are essentially healthy.* The reason for this is that when you are just learning, you will make mistakes—we all do. You might inadvertently raise energy that needs to be grounded, or suppress energy that is struggling to rise. If the person you are working with is healthy, they will have the resilience to bounce back from these temporary shifts; if they aren't, without meaning to, you can do harm. So even if someone who is ill requests a session, please resist, and encourage them to instead work with a health practitioner who has already developed expertise in their field—they can always come back to you when they feel better. If you practice diligently, over time you too will develop the necessary expertise to help people heal from illness.

On Buying Your Instruments

Usually when people first start learning about the sacred healing instruments, they can hardly wait to run out and purchase their own set. But if you are working with this system, it is important to get the best quality and the right types of bowls to work with. It is better to start with just a few bowls and build your set over time as you integrate information and become more educated about why you need each bowl and what it is used for. I will work with you personally to help you through this process. You can reach me through my website: tibetanbowlschool.com.

Sound healing is an exciting field, with limitless potential for helping people discover their diamond selves—as I did during that first session so long ago—and achieve wholeness, harmony, and healing along the way. I am thrilled to be able to introduce you to its principles and techniques. So let's begin!

Part I

Fundamentals of Sound Healing

In the first section of the book I will introduce you to the fundamental principles of sound healing. Chapter 1 offers an orientation to the healing process and your role in it. Chapter 2 covers an essential element of a sound healing session that may surprise you (hint: it doesn't involve the instruments at all). And in Chapter 3, I'll give you an overview of the elements of a good sound healing session.

Chapter 1
FRAMEWORKS FOR ILLNESS AND HEALING

If we accept that sound is vibration and we know that vibration touches every part of our physical being, then we understand that sound is heard not only through our ears but through every cell in our bodies. One reason sound heals on a physical level is because it so deeply touches and transforms us on the emotional and spiritual planes. Sound can redress imbalances on every level of physiologic functioning and can play a positive role in the treatment of virtually any medical disorder.

DR. MITCHEL GAYNOR, former director of medical oncology and integrative medicine, Strang Cancer Prevention Center Institute[i]

To get you started on your journey to becoming a sound healing practitioner, let's first establish a general framework for understanding this unique healing modality. In this chapter we'll look at the nature of healing itself. We'll also explore how the sacred sound instruments work to shift energy and effect change. And we'll cover the all-important healing partnership between practitioner and client and discuss your role in that equation.

What Is Healing?

There are many ways to think about healing.

One way is to consider two contrasting views: healing as a "cure"—an ending or final result—or as a process that is infinite.

Webster's defines the former, finite sense as "the complete biological resolution of a diseased state" and "the elimination of disease, distress, evil." But when viewed as an ongoing process, several other definitions come to mind:

- To make or become whole; the mending of a breach
- To free from grief, troubles, evil
- To become well or healthy again
- Restoring to health or soundness
- One of my favorite definitions of healing is this one by Jeanne Achterberg: "An intuitive perception of the universe and all its inhabitants as being of one fabric"[1]

A Return to the Wholeness of the Self

From my perspective, no matter what kind of illness or imbalance one is dealing with, healing is a path back to the self. By "self" I mean the divine self, the *diamond self*—our essence, the energetic presence we came into the world with that is and will always remain whole and intact despite external circumstances. As such, healing is a *spiritual awakening* that impacts the physical body.

As a practitioner, you will guide and witness this awakening, which gives a lot of validation to your client's experience. You will help them feel their wholeness and connect with source, to see that their own unique perfection is that sense of themselves as an energetic light being. You will help them experience who they are outside of their roles, their jobs, their relationships, their positions, and their possessions and recognize their still point where everything is right and well. The skilled healer will help the client expand their relationship with their higher self into more and more of their experience so they can take that sense of wholeness and bring it to their day, to their family, and to their work and delight in how little successes build on each other very quickly.

From Disharmony to Harmony

Another way of looking at healing is to see it as the movement from disharmony or discord to harmony. This journey toward harmony includes the ability to perceive one's self and one's situation from and within a much larger perspective: a movement from duality to nonduality (divine awareness or enlightenment). This is the spiritual awakening I speak of that has consequences for our physical well-being. As we awaken, our perspective shifts. As our perspective shifts, our vibration shifts. As our vibration shifts, our cellular makeup shifts. These changes cannot occur separately in the various aspects of ourselves; they affect the whole of who we are and extend infinitely.

Like many healers, I believe that illness is a manifestation of disharmony within the body—an imbalance in the cells or in a given organ—and that healing can be achieved by restoring the normal vibratory frequencies of the diseased, out-of-harmony parts of the body. Vibrational healing, especially with sound, is a potent way of doing this.

Sound pioneer and gong master Richard Rudis explains this another way:

> The fundamental state of the universe is a state of bliss. Our core state, because we are part of the natural universe, is also one of bliss and great ease. When we disconnect from our core state through stress, distraction, illness, and the challenges of daily life, dis-ease occurs—spiritual, physical, and mental.

I see matter as energy vibrating at various rates. By altering the rate of vibration, we can change the structure of matter. The most effective healing sounds are those of high frequency such as those produced by the Himalayan bowls. They gently nudge us back to our natural state of bliss.[2]

Healing into the Universe—and Love

So, healing is a process in which we are released from an ego-centered, finite perspective of ourselves in the world and move into our essence, where our vibratory energy is connected with the universe. On a biological level, the sacred sound instruments affect a great deal of physical change, but sacred sound healing has far-reaching implications that occur on emotional and spiritual levels as well. This is a regenerative process married to a spiritual awakening that can have profound consequences on illness, disease, and all aspects of our lives.

My work has confirmed over and over again that *any specific illness is an indicator of which door to open to access love—of which area is most in need of love.* The illness is the path to love; the healing crisis we created, consciously or unconsciously, can catapult us into awakening and attending to our profound needs. Without the illness or crisis we would continue to avoid that part of ourselves.

A Healing Analogy

Long ago, as a master's degree student, I did a lot of training and development work, and one of the things I learned about was how groups form. Whenever you join a new group, whatever kind of group it is (culture, family, job, school), there is a series of four developmental stages.

The first one, *forming,* is kind of the honeymoon stage where things seem new and interesting. The second part, *storming,* is where things don't happen the way you think they should or you want them to, and everything is a challenge. There is a diminishing of normal functions in this new environment. The third stage, *norming,* is getting into the flow of things and figuring out what works. The final stage, *performing,* is where you are effectively interacting within the new context.

I think the stages of healing are similar, minus the honeymoon stage, and it is helpful to recognize which stage you're in. Are you at the cosmic whack-in-the-head stage because of a car accident, illness, divorce, or job loss? All those things can be experienced as trauma, a wake-up call, and an opportunity to get back into balance.

Are you in the stage of a diminishing of normal functions, where everything seems to be working against you? You notice that you're forgetting things, or all of a sudden you're crying all the time, or you've got diarrhea, and you just can't do what you normally do because that cosmic whack-in-the-head, in whatever form, is impacting your body/mind and how you walk through space and time. With illness, this is where people start feeling betrayed by their body and environment.

It is important that practitioners recognize these stages because even just naming them can be helpful. The practitioner can help the client come to a perspective about the condition that says, *"This condition you are in now is here to help you gain perspective on some aspect of your life that you've really been ignoring. You may not feel or look good, but that doesn't mean you are bad. The illness may not be betraying you at all—in fact, it may be leading you to something better."*

In development work, norming and performing start to happen when the person accepts the situation and works with rather than against it. Healing is often uncomfortable, and one belief system that gets in the way of the healing process is the idea that everything has to work in a particular way to be understood as healing (for example, that *it isn't supposed to be painful*).

Those who have suffered illness for a long time are also often in the situation of needing to release something that has become like a friend, albeit a painful one. There's also the fear of not knowing what to replace the pain with; what will fill the space the illness has taken up for so long?

So, after the cosmic whack-in-the-head, diminishing of normal functions, and betrayal of the body, people come to you and hope you will fix them.

An external fix will only go so far, but you can use your amazing sound tools and skills to help them become a partner with you in their healing, and then the healer of their own life.

How the Instruments Heal

The sound vibrations of the instruments you will be working with—the tingshas, the ganta and dorje, and the bowls—bring us to the part of ourselves that remembers on a visceral level that we don't need an excuse to heal, that in fact we are divine beings. Their sound helps us remember experientially who we really are. And when we "get" that, when we feel ourselves to be the diamond self, we know that the only way to be with self is through unconditional love and self-care. We know we don't need a reason or an illness to justify complete, self-respecting, loving nurturing. We recognize that we have been enslaved and seduced into the illusion that we are not perfect. Sound *stops* this illusion, the mind chatter, the misconceptions, and puts us directly back into alignment with the universal flow of perfection that is our true nature.

Because we learn through repetition, as we repeat our experience with the instruments we anchor ourselves in the memory of well-being until it replaces the illusion of illness. Our body is the vessel through which the frequency of perfection is transmitted; it is also the transmitter.

In Tibetan Buddhism the bowls are seen as transmitting the dharma—the teachings of the Buddha, including the thinking and behaviors that make up the central principles of Buddhist philosophy—and in particular, manifestations of the Voidness teaching. Richard Rudis explains:

> In the words of the great Tibetan master Bodhisattva Gwalwa Karmapa, the singing bowls of Tibet emit the "Sound of the Void," the sound of the universe manifesting. They are a symbol of the unknowable and as an alloy date back to the Buddha Shakyamuni (560–480 BC). Their origins and detailed histories are shrouded in the distant past and are

surely a gift from the shamanistic Bon religion that precedes Buddhism in Tibet by centuries. For centuries they have been utilized for healing and consciousness transformation. We are now discovering the science behind this powerful ancient modality that is so effective for healing today. Modern medicine can now measure and thus confirm the practice of sound as a means to heal.[3]

The Voidness teachings say that nothing exists apart from anything else. The false perception that one exists as an independent entity is one of the basic causes of suffering and illness. Everything is interconnected and everything we think, see, feel, and do has an impact on everything else. This concept can be a bit daunting to truly internalize, but help is at hand. The bowls are here as compassionate ambassadors of the Truth, gently nudging us into the memory of this Truth.

The sound vibrations of the bowls break down our ability to maintain our ego boundaries. As we release our sense of "self," we enter into the universal flow of energy. In fact, we are always there, but we spend most of our time trying to define ourselves as apart from or independent of it.

While we are in that universal flow, we have a sense of timelessness, of floating, of release from our physical bodies. We seem to drift off into another place, and it takes some time to fully reenter our body after being exposed to the bowls' sounds. Often it is only after we finally release into the universal flow that we realize how much stress we have been maintaining in order to function as an independent entity.

The Innate Nature of the Instruments

In the Tibetan Buddhist tradition, we are working with the interrelationship of all things and the innate nature of the instruments. What they actually do, as I have said, is bring us back into the visceral, experiential memory of our wholeness. How much does that count in the greater scheme of things? When you're looking at specific illnesses or challenges and working with an instrument that brings your client back into a memory of wholeness, think about how that can help them get in touch with something that is *not* their pain body. What relief!

The instruments bring us into alignment. Think of this metaphor: Imagine just one of the spinal vertebrae being out of alignment. How many peripheral aspects are impacted by that? Organs will be impacted. The emotional body will be frustrated by discomfort. Muscles will be tense around that vertebra, which may impact the nerves. There can be inflammation. That one vertebra will be felt on many different levels.

Bring that one vertebra back into alignment and what happens with all the peripheral parts of the body? That's how I think of the instruments. Handled correctly, they will create an energetic alignment that affects all aspects of the person: physical, mental, emotional, and spiritual. Of course, there are many things to do to focus on one specific area of need or another, but it's also important to keep in mind what is happening in general.

On a purely physical level, when the instruments are played correctly, they balance the left and the right hemispheres of the brain, regulate blood pressure, and create cardiorespiratory synchrony where all systems begin to dance together. That creates within us an effective environment for healing from whatever is derailing our system.

Sympathetic Resonance

Sound healing makes use of the phenomenon of sympathetic resonance. Science tells us that all life is energy. Further, this energy is eternal, constantly changing form. Each "energy shape" has its own particular pattern of frequencies or vibrations. When one form of energy experiences the matching frequency of a musical note, it will vibrate in sympathy with the note in *sympathetic resonance.*

A strong enough sound vibration can even cause a form to restructure itself, as has been noted with cancer cells (see Fabien Maman's work)[4] and water crystals. In his book *The Hidden Messages in Water,* Japanese doctor and researcher Masaru Emoto includes photographs showing the impact of the vibrations of consciousness on the formulation of water crystals.[5] Considering that our bodies are largely composed of water, you can imagine how similar restructuring could be effected throughout our system by sound vibration. Opera singers have shattered crystal glasses by creating and intensifying matching frequencies—again, the restructuring impact of sympathetic resonance.

The high-frequency sounds of the Himalayan bowls gently nudge us back to our natural state of bliss. They emit the sound "AUM," the frequency of which is the vibration of universal perfection. When we are exposed to that frequency over time, we fall into sympathetic resonance with it.

The Vagus Nerve: Entryway to the Entire System

The vagus nerve is key to how the instruments do their work. It is the only nerve that travels from the brain stem and accesses, stimulates, sends energy to, and brings information from every major organ in the body except the spleen. The "antennas" of the vagus nerves are in the ears. This is why the head triad, a fundamental configuration of bowls that you will read about later in the book, is so important for maintaining that soothing, regular information, that balancing sound. The vibrations from the bowls travel from the inner ear all the way through the nervous system.

We're really working with the energy body and accessing the physical body through sound. The instruments do their job and the body receives the sound and very effectively transmits it. As the sounds travel through the vagus nerve and go through the different parts of the system, they carry soothing energy, balancing energy, or enhancing energy throughout the body.

Playing Versus Healing

I would like to make one last point about how the instruments heal before we move on to discussing the healing partnership between practitioner and client: there is a big difference between playing bowls and healing with sound. In healing work, you are slowly and gently guiding your client into a trance state (an alpha/theta brain-wave state) where they experience higher states of consciousness and healing. You are working with their cellular memory, changing old patterns to new ones, and establishing the memory of wellness within them by creating and repeating healing patterns. This is why it is so important to use high-quality instruments and attain mastery in how to play them effectively using the elements of placement, volume, pace, rhythm, patterning, and intention.

Healing Is a Partnership

The sound healing process requires a partnership between practitioner and client. Healing means creating an equal balance between receiving and giving. A lot of people see healing as something that's happening *to* them and don't realize that healing is the whole process that is happening *through* them, and the issue is what they are doing with it.

Many people would prefer a fast-track pill to the collaborative work of sound healing, but there is no pill that can effect the multifaceted shifting toward health that this modality offers. Many clients throw their power away in the attempt to make the practitioner responsible for their healing. Yet this is a futile and often costly endeavor, for each of us is our own inner healer. The practitioner's purpose is simply to guide us back to that awareness. The sound healing client has to take ownership of their own role, to be a witness to and participant in their own healing.

So our goal is to help people gain the realization that they're responsible for their healing. Along the way, they're going to feel depression, loss of hope, despondency, anger, sadness, and fatigue—all of those nuances of life that you, as a compassionate witness, help them navigate through. They can accept what depression feels like but realize *they* are not depression. Through your help, they can see the areas of their lives that *are* working and gain a larger perspective. They trust that you are going to stand with them but they also need to stand for themselves. They must develop the courage to not run away from a situation, but rather to experience what it feels like, accept it, and then transmute it. *You cannot get rid of something that you don't own.*

Following is a general breakdown of the responsibilities of each side of the healing equation.

Practitioner Responsibilities

- Gain mastery in utilizing the instruments.
- Experience self-transformation with the bowls.
- Prepare for sessions and create a sacred space.
- Serve as a facilitator and witness to the healing process.
- Serve as a compassionate mirror to help the client become aware of self-sabotaging behaviors, belief systems, and words.
- Support the client as master healer.
- Keep accurate records.

Practice Partner or Client Responsibilities

- Acknowledge the damage they do to themselves when they accept stress (see the chart on the effects of stress on brain and body, Appendix E, page 247).
- Accept responsibility for changing the attitudes, beliefs, and conditions that contribute to stress.
- Devote enough time to strengthen the energetic and spiritual systems that replace stress with nourishment.
- Take power versus giving away power.
- Create strong and clear intentions and affirmations.
- Open to the reality that healing is not always comfortable.

The Seduction of the Ego

Be forewarned: your ego will want you to take responsibility for doing the healing—to see yourself as a great and powerful healer. Don't fall for it. If you allow this to happen, you are really using your client to validate the part of you that lacks confidence. Your real power lies in becoming skillful at raising your vibration, playing the instruments, and hearing their information, observing your client, and serving as a compassionate witness to their process. Of course, you may always provide them with your thoughts about what you are seeing and what they are experiencing. But these must be presented in a manner that will deepen their work with themselves rather than their reliance on you.

More on the Practitioner's Role

The healing process means you must keep your own energy high, be an effective witness, and be skilled in how you play the instruments. The work with different ailments requires your ability to know how to access what is needed. Is it talk? Is it hands on? What is it that will help each person be able to recognize him- or herself? For some people, it's a lot of bowl work. For some people, it's ganta work. For others, it's hands on or a mixture of techniques. Some people can make a big shift in one session, and from then on the work is strengthening that shift. Whichever techniques you use, it is vital to not only keep the person's wholeness and wellness in your own mind but to reflect that back for them to see.

When we talk about the interrelationship of all things in terms of healing, that doesn't mean that as practitioners we have to do everything all the time, but we have to know that healing is a combination of many different activities. It covers the range from dispersing, grounding, and soothing a dysfunction on one end of the spectrum to strengthening the wellness experience on the other.

Creating the "Envelope"

Now, at this stage I am going to tell you a little secret: *You don't really do any healing. Your practice partners and future clients will heal themselves.* A seasoned practitioner knows that it is the client's own wisdom that has brought them to the session, and that same wisdom will provide the healing. You are simply the facilitator of their process, the witness, and the support system.

This might bring up a question for you: Why do I need to go through all this training if I don't do any healing? The answer is important for you to understand because otherwise you can get very confused, work according to your own agenda, or let your ego get involved. Let me explain:

Healing takes place in a specific context. In our case, it is within the context of vibrational sound. People will seek you out because something in them *knows* that vibrational sound contains a key to their well-being. The trouble is, they don't know how to best create the sounds. You *do*—or at least you will. The *sound* you generate is the important thing, not *you yourself.* When your clients experience the right sounds and patterns and you are there as a facilitator and witness to this experience, they can access their own inner healer.

Your clients need to understand this as well. If they look to *you* as the healer—not accepting their role in the partnership that I outlined earlier—they place healing outside of themselves and are not really participants in their own health. If this happens, healing cannot take place to its fullest extent and you may both be disappointed.

Your purpose, then, is to provide the right context, or "envelope," to serve as a conduit for your client's inner healer. As you gain skill and mastery as a facilitator and player of the instruments, you will create better and better context for your clients' inner healers to perform their work. But from the very first session, be sure to let your practice partners in on this important principle of sound healing—set the right expectations from the very start.

Shifting Belief Systems

On the path of healing, the task of the practitioner is to help the client shift their perspective of themselves. People often hold strong belief systems that they are unaware of. Remember: sound means all sound, not just the instruments. It includes our voice, our conversations, self-talk, the inner recording that's playing. The practitioner's job is to help raise the client's awareness of what they're doing to and with themselves, and in so doing empower them to release ineffective patterns and create self-sustaining ones. This work helps create a shift of attitude and a reconnection with a place of inner peace, leading to hope, power, and inspiration.

People tend to focus on their weakest link, and they identify with it. *"I have cancer, that's who I am. I am cancer. I am walking cancer."* There is no acknowledgment that they are breathing and eating, have great eyesight and a roof over their head, are a parent, or are creative. Many things are working just fine but they completely take those things for granted.

If someone is forgetful, that's how they see themselves. *"I am walking forgetfulness, and I'm so forgetful that I can't even remember that I got up this morning, went to work, did the laundry, went grocery shopping, and made dinner for my family.*" But the fact is, you need memory to do any of those things. It's up to us to help people find that sense of perspective. Perspective is so important in the healing process. It gets people out of the position of being victims of life and shifts them to the position of being witnesses to life. As soon as you do that, everything starts to get better.

So let's say you're working with depression or anger. What you are really working with is the belief that *"I am unworthy, I'm trash"* and shifting that to *"I am worthy."* On some level, I think all illness is about that message and that shift. We strive to transform the view of self from being less than whole, or partially damaged goods, to one of where the person can see who they are as they are and then expand that love energy not just outward, but inward to embrace their totality.

Shining a Light on Toleration

One of the things I find to be a major cause of illness and stress, and something you might not necessarily think about, is toleration: unfinished business that is taking up psychic and energetic space.

For some people it might be putting up with a behavior from a family member, friend, or coworker whom they dislike but feel powerless to change. For others it could be self-critical thoughts that get in the way of accomplishing or just being as they would prefer to be (for example, relaxed and present). It can be something like a messy desk, poor eating habits, extra weight, or procrastination. It could be tolerating a condition, such as your car's tires wearing out: *I know that they need changing. Every time I go out, I think I'm going to have an accident.*

An important aspect of chatting with a client before a session is to help that person recognize the things they are tolerating in their life that do not serve them, things they're carrying around like a bag on their back. Most of us tolerate things unconsciously. We sort of know that we are, but until we have a witness to declare to, we don't do anything about it.

So when you're looking at patterns and belief systems, understand that tolerations are patterns, and in order to make space for healing, you must interrupt those ineffective patterns and replace them with healing intention.

Getting to the Root Cause

When a person comes in with an ailment, it's likely they will want to feel assured that you will work with that problem directly. If they say, "I have swelling here," and you work with the swelling, there's a sense of safety in that. Their belief system might be telling them that this swelling comes, for example, from too much working on the computer. And it very well might, but something else is going on too—and you need to address that root cause.

What makes someone work past the point where their body is tired, where they feel restriction and pain? There is a taskmaster in there somewhere who is circumventing that person's awareness of their inner messages and pushing them past their limits. So even though their carpal tunnel syndrome may come from overworking a certain physical area, there is something underneath that, and as sound healers, our effectiveness is predicated on the ability to get under it too.

A little further on you'll read a chapter on how to craft effective affirmations. When you co-create with your client the exact right words of affirmation that address their core issue, they will often have a physical reaction—a release of some kind. It might be tears, a movement of breath, or a vocalization, but whatever form it takes, it is evidence that something deep has been shifted. These signals help you identify the core issue, but the most vital tool in getting to the root is your ability to listen deeply, with your ears, your eyes, and all your senses, the same way you listen for subtle shifts of sound in the instruments.

Accent Work

The reality is that even though most of the work you do during a session will impact the area the client is concerned about—because it addresses the root cause—the person might still think, *Gosh, I told her I had a pain in my thigh and she didn't directly work exactly where I told her I had that pain*. And they might feel somehow short-changed. This is where what I call *accent work* comes in. For the benefit of the client's belief system that's telling them "If my thigh hurts, we need to work on my thigh," you will want to focus some of your work on that area.

The Role of Intention in Sound Healing

My experience has shown me that people make great shifts when their subconscious mind and cellular memory come into alignment with their consciousness. So, after several sessions with a client, when I feel that trust has been well established and they are in a deeply relaxed state, I introduce words and/or visualizations that support their healing intention. While they are in the altered state of consciousness the instruments create, their mind is open to such suggestions. In this state, too, the cellular memory that often holds on to pain and suffering can be softened and altered by suggestion and intention.

As practitioners we can help people define and then validate their experience by giving them the words to use to describe what they're feeling and sensing, as a way to guide them to discover their own stillness and connection to their own divinity. They may not have words for this at first, but once they know what it is, they know what it feels like to feel connected and they know that they've been validated. And then they can go back to that place more easily.

You will find instruction for expressing intention as an affirmation in Chapter 2. But for a visual depiction of the effects of intention on matter, take a look at these before-and-after photographs of a cotton cell, first enriched with prayer only and then with both prayer and sound vibrations. While it doesn't involve playing the instruments at all, this illustrates why intention can be one of the most powerful tools the sound healer can use to create healing shifts in energy.

Cotton before Prayer

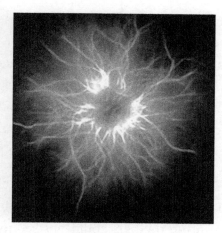

Cotton with Prayer

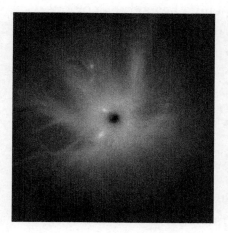

Cotton before Prayer and Sound

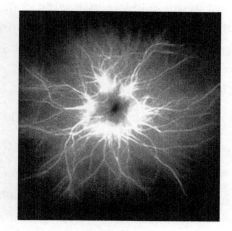

Cotton with Prayer and Sound

Photos by French sound practitioner Fabien Maman, who founded Tama Do, the Academy of Sound, Color and Movement, in California. Copyright Fabien Maman, 1981.

To Know Without Reason or Logic: Using Intuition

Intuition is seeing with the soul.

DEAN KOONTZ

Intuition plays an important part in a sound healing session, so I want to include some thoughts about intuition in this framework. Conducting a technically correct layout has great value, but without the guidance of your intuition, your healing sessions will lack a key ingredient.

Intuition will help guide your choices during a session, so it is well worth your time to gain some skill and confidence in accessing it. Intuition will also keep you from falling into the following practitioner traps:

- Taking on the conditions of the clients you treat
- Trying to fix the situation (having an agenda), rather than simply creating the best container for healing to occur
- Not knowing which clients to work with, and not to work with
- Not being able to sense what is happening beyond the obvious
- Working from a foundation of mind or ego
- Being confused as to what to do during a session

Strengthening Your Intuition

To strengthen intuition, first develop your personal foundation:

- Clear your own karma through introspection and energy work with others.
- Meet your own physical and emotional needs.
- Know your values and stay in your integrity.
- Meditate.
- Detach from the outcome.
- Learn to witness rather than interpreting or judging.

Act as if following your intuition is natural, as if everything around you holds clues and you trust those messages. Spend time witnessing yourself during the day to develop more awareness of your own tendencies and change them if needed. Here I'm referring to such tendencies as second-guessing yourself, negative self-talk, or shaming yourself when you make a mistake.

Each individual has a unique way of experiencing intuition. Intuitive information may be auditory, kinesthetic, or visual. Some of the signs people report that tell them their intuition is at work include a heavy feeling in the gut or heart, contracted muscles, weakened knees, dreams, an "aha" moment, the flash of an image, or the flow of things in a specific direction. Intuition comes as a feeling, hunch, insight, random thought, small voice, sensation, or inkling. We know it is happening through synchronicity or a flash of inspiration. Some of the textures of intuition include a feeling of effortlessness, an "it just feels right" sense of elation, a persistent sensation or impression, or an attraction to a thought or feeling—a kind of pull or tug. Intuition doesn't normally feel desperate, urgent, charged with emotion, or demanding of effort. It does not bring us out of integrity, and it is not a result of analysis.

I encourage you to invite intuition, honor its presence, engage in some journaling, and spend focused time developing your awareness and skills in this area. Over time your trust in your intuition will strengthen and it will become one of your most powerful allies.

Intuition Exercise

Here is an exercise you can try. For one week, keep a writing pad with you at all times. Record in it each time you perceive an intuition and note how it came to you (as a vision, a thought, a gut feeling, or something else). Also note when you are confused about whether something that arises is intuitive or based in thought or ego. In doing this you will be able to fine-tune your sensitivity to your intuition and increase your confidence in it.

Working with Symbolism

It is beyond the scope of this book to look at symbolism in depth, but if you allow yourself to muse upon any part of the body or any illness, you can often come upon what it may symbolize—and that can give you very helpful context to guide your healing sessions. So I invite you to take some time to write down various parts of the body and the physical task of that part or organ, and then let yourself imagine what that symbolizes. For example, what can joint issues indicate? Joints are about mobility—movement from up to down and side to side. If there are joint problems, is there a rigidness of perspective somewhere? Or a fear of moving from a stuck situation?

Louise Hay's wonderful *You Can Heal Your Life* lists the symbolism of many physical issues and is a great resource to help you gain another perspective on what is happening in the body.

A Note on Knowing Your Limits

For a final note on your role as practitioner, I want to briefly point out that you need to know the limits of your skills and abilities, particularly when it comes to helping people process the issues that arise when a healing shift takes place. You will quickly discover that a sound healing session can create a whole host of responses in your clients. Sometimes when you're working at the throat, for example, issues with the third chakra will come up (for much more on chakras, see part III). The person may know that they need to talk to someone about those issues, but may not know how to voice or deal with them. If you feel this is something you are not equipped to handle, it is perfectly appropriate to refer the individual to someone else, such as a counselor or a therapist. You don't need to do it all yourself.

If you have had some training in role playing, however, you can use it to work with these issues. I have been trained, so I'm comfortable doing it. But even for me, there are some issues I won't touch. If someone comes to me with a heroin addiction, for instance, that's too big. I'll refer them to an addiction specialist because that will be most helpful to them.

So while you are learning the ins and outs of creating an effective healing environment and working with the instruments, also be mindful of and honest about your own capabilities and what you have to offer at this stage of your sound healing education. Contribute your support where you can, and refer people to people with specific expertise where appropriate.

In closing this chapter, I want to leave you with a key takeaway: we are not our condition. We are far greater and more powerful than any external condition—we are eternal. Sound healing presents us with a path to examine our attitudes, beliefs, and behaviors, raise our consciousness and vibrational frequency, and ultimately make changes in our lives that provide a strong foundation for well-being.

Chapter 2
Intention, Affirmation, and Transformation

If you touch one thing with deep awareness, you touch everything.

Thich Nhat Hanh

I mentioned the importance of intention in the first chapter on frameworks for illness and healing, and it is so key to sound healing that I want to cover it next. It is really an essential component of sound healing because adding intention to the frequency of the bowls powerfully increases their healing potential. Turn back to Fabien Maman's photographs on page 23 and notice how much the energy of the cotton cell expanded with the combination of prayer (positive intention) and sound vibrations. Now you have a visual sense of the potential of these two forms of vibration when used in combination. You will be a more effective sound healer if you take the time and effort to build your intention skills.

An Exercise in Intention

You can start with an exercise based on one in Dr. Masaru Emoto's book *The Hidden Messages in Water*. It demonstrates the power of intention—the power *you* innately possess to influence and shift energy and matter.

> Find a small to mid-size cloud in the sky. Now direct a beam of energy from your consciousness to that cloud with the intention of breaking it up into smaller pieces. As you do this, repeat, as if it has already happened, "The cloud has disappeared." At the same time, say to your consciousness, "Thank you for doing that," again as if it has already happened. When your intention is fully engaged, in only a few moments, the cloud will be gone.[1]

You may be skeptical: I can break a cloud into pieces using only my intention? I can assure you it is something you can do. I erased the clouds from an entire section of sky the first time I tried this.

Be patient with yourself with this exercise, because you will be learning what the texture of pure intention is—a huge lesson. If you are attached to the outcome or try too hard, this will prevent you from directing your energy and you will not be able to do it. Also, engage your belief—*believe* that when you do this exercise, the cloud will disappear.

Intention + Attention = Manifestation

Now I want to say something about illness that may stir up some strong emotions: *most people would not recognize the degree of focused self-care it takes to heal from life-threatening illness or chronic conditions if they had not contracted the illness in the first place.*

It is often the lack of this degree of attention to self-care that, on some level, causes illness. Illness is an uncomfortable but *acceptable* reason to focus on yourself without guilt—or with less guilt than you would feel if you had no health challenges. The transformation from illness to healing occurs as we are able to direct our loving, compassionate energy toward ourselves *(intention)*, when and as we need it *(attention)*, without guilt, shame, or surrendering to the inner critic.

The Healing Intention

In the altered state of consciousness that sound healing creates, the mind is open to suggestion, and the cellular memory that often holds on to pain and suffering can be softened and altered. But you need to know how to create effective wording for suggestions. When you have an energy healing practice, it's important that crafting strong affirmations becomes second nature for you because moving energy is subtle business. Your exact choice of words impacts the energy, so you want to get it right.

You can start learning how to do that now.

Creating an Effective Intention: Craft an Affirmation

Intention can take the form of prayer, chanting, and even silent focused attention, but declaring your intention aloud using an affirmation is best. To do this, follow this simple two-step process:

First, decide on your intention. What do you want to have happen? Then create the related affirmation:

- Make it simple, specific, clear, positive, and concise.
- Put it in the present moment as if it is already happening ("I *am*" versus "I want, wish, need, hope, or should").
- Eliminate any of those future-oriented words like "want, wish, need, hope and should."

Once you have expressed your intention in this way, you have an affirmation. Here are a few examples of intentions and the positive affirmations you could create to manifest the intention:

Intention: "I want to get rid of this stress."

Affirmation: "I feel peaceful, balanced, and content with my life."

Intention: "I want to get off these pain killers and *stop* feeling tired."

Affirmation: "My body feels healthy, vibrant with energy, and strong. I nourish myself only with the things that support my highest well-being."

Intention: "I want to be open to abundance and be able to feel financially stable."

Affirmation: "I have more than enough money, financial stability, and joy in my life to take care of all my needs and desires."

Your Turn

I invite you to take a break from reading right now and do this exercise for yourself. Then you will have an immediate understanding of what makes for a strong affirmation, and you'll be well on your way to helping your clients create their own positive and effective affirmations.

When you have finished, share your message with close friends or colleagues to get their thoughts. This takes some practice, and their feedback can help.

> Begin by writing down—*without editing*—the transformations you want to see. You don't have to worry about the words yet; the important thing is to capture your thoughts. Then take your list and replace anything negative with a positive. Take out words such as "want," "wish," "should," "need," and "hope" and replace them with "am" or "choose to." Then condense your message into one or two short sentences that are in the present moment.

A Word About Framing Affirmations in the Present Moment

Wording your affirmations in the present moment directs the energy to the "now" rather than to a past or future moment, neither of which actually exists. This sets into motion the energetic wheel of synchronicity that will manifest your intention. This doesn't mean you don't have to do anything and you can just wait for things to happen. It works because when you affirm in the present moment, your actions more easily line up with your desire. It means that you position yourself as the active magnet that engages with life in a manner that is more aligned with what you want, thus creating more space and opportunity for your desires to materialize. When you direct your attention to an affirmation, you will naturally start taking the action steps needed to realize your dream or goal.

If this feels awkward at first—in other words, if declaring something that isn't happening yet feels false to you—let me assure you that it is worth getting past the awkwardness. When you place the affirmation in the present moment, you are energizing and nourishing it. And that is exactly what is needed for it to manifest.

Preparing to Work with Others

How would you invite a practice partner to create an intention and affirmation for their healing session? Once you feel like you're on track in crafting affirmations for yourself, the next step is to prepare to help other people do the same. What words would you use to help someone else formulate an effective intention?

The first thing to do is to pass along the "secrets" of a strong affirmation that I outlined earlier. Invite them to: make it simple, specific, clear, positive, and concise; frame it in the present moment as if it is already happening; and eliminate future-oriented wording like "want" or "should."

Also let them know this: *everything they need is already within them.* Tell them they can add a variation of this statement to their affirmation if they wish. Take a look at the two affirmations that follow and you will see how you can add the truth that everything you need is already within. It is often helpful to start with a strong positive statement and then take it to a deeper level.

Affirmation: I feel peaceful, balanced, and content with my life.

Going deeper: I am connected to the peace that already resides within me.

Affirmation: I have more than enough financial stability and joy in my life to take care of all my needs and desires.

Going deeper: I am connected to abundance, which already resides within me.

Your Turn

Creating effective affirmations is all about practice, so please take some more time to do that now. Using the guidelines I have outlined in this chapter, use your imagination and consider healing issues you have encountered or might encounter with your practice partners. Create five to ten new affirmations:

- First, write down a likely intention—the healing results your practice partner might want to see. Use the words this person would probably use in expressing their desires to you.
- Now shift the wording so it is positive and present oriented.

The more experience you have in creating affirmations, the easier it is to do it in a sound healing setting. So practice this until you feel very comfortable creating these powerful healing tools, and can do so quickly.

Use Affirmations Often

It is key that we give ourselves enough cues to bombard our environment with them so we can shift the thought. Why? Because what we're used to is so ingrained that it's easy to go back to old habits. A concerted effort to create new habits is necessary. An affirmation is a cue, a reminder to keep you focused on your goal and to help attract that goal to you. It neutralizes the negative self-talk. Repetition also keeps you focused on your goal until you find yourself taking active steps toward the new vision of yourself the affirmation paints for you.

How do you bombard yourself with cues? Place affirmations wherever you will see them regularly: on your mirror, on the fridge door, or in your car, for example.

If Affirmations Aren't Working . . .

Let's talk about your own affirmations for yourself. If the affirmations you have created don't seem to be helping you move forward, it's probably because of one of three things:

- Lack of patience. You get impatient and negative about your affirmations when things don't move along as fast as you want. But remember: you don't have the ability to make this contract with the universe: "Okay, universe, I'm doing all the right things and so I want to see change happen within my time frame." That's not how the universe works. There are no contracts. So do all the right things and say the right words because it's the right thing to do, period. It's when you have no ulterior motive that things begin to shift. If you're holding out for a contract, the universe is going to really make you sweat it out. Patience and trust are what you need here.
- Attachment to future outcomes. Sometimes you can be so attached to shifts happening in a certain way that you don't recognize all the other opportunities that cross your path. That's why it's so important to hold the vision while also staying in the present moment.
- Distraction. If you get distracted from your affirmation and don't give it the necessary amount of repetition, you diminish its power. That's why I encourage you to bombard your environment with reminders. The world is full of distractions, and it's very easy to forget an affirmation unless you are reminded of it many times during the day.

Now that you have some grounding in the role of affirmations in sound healing and have had a chance to practice creating them, to round out our discussion of fundamentals it's time to learn how a session typically unfolds—the "anatomy" of a sound healing session. That's the subject of Chapter 3.

Chapter 3
ANATOMY OF A SOUND HEALING SESSION

Healing is a spiritual awakening that impacts the physical body.
Sound is the train that gets you there.

So far in this book, you have learned some important principles of illness and healing. You have also learned how to create effective healing affirmations—a basic building block of a good sound healing session—and gotten some practice doing that. You may be wondering, *When do I get to learn about the sacred sound instruments and how to use them?* Rest assured, we'll get there—in the very next section of the book, in fact. But first there is one more step. I want to give you a general orientation to what I think of as the basic "anatomy" of a sound healing session, the general outline of how a session typically opens and closes. This way, you will have a sense of the flow of a session in mind when you start learning how to use the instruments. You will already have a general road map for your first practice sessions.

First, Raise Your Own Vibration

It may come as a surprise that your sound healing session begins before your practice partner even knocks on the door. It starts with raising *your* vibration. What do I mean by this, and why is it so important? Well, sound healing takes place in a context of high-frequency vibration. The sound of the sacred instruments offer such a vibration, but you can greatly add to their effectiveness by raising your own vibration.

This is important for two reasons: it creates a protective energetic shield around you, and it allows the energy of the instruments to flow through you without interference. This is why part of your preparation must always include the practice of raising your own vibration before your client arrives. This is what allows for *presencing;* that is, being in the moment, with no personal agenda of your own for the client's healing journey. (More on Presencing follows shortly.)

How do you raise your vibration? Many techniques can work, including a short meditation, sitting in silence, chanting, or deep energetic breathing. I encourage you to experiment on your own, but this is my favorite way:

- Get into a low squat with your heels on the ground.
- Feel your feet firmly planted on the ground.
- Place your elbows between your knees and push outward.
- Bring breath into the lowest part of your belly.
- Now, as slowly and fully as possible, bring breath into your entire body, expanding it upward from the lower abdomen into the head.
- Now exhale completely, pushing all the air out.
- Repeat this several times, or until you feel cleared and grounded.

Now you are ready to welcome your practice partner.

Opening a Session

When a person first walks through your door for a session, you want the space they are entering to be welcoming and exude safety, so set up the physical space with care. One sign that you have succeeded is if a person sighs deeply upon entering the space.

Invite your practice partner to sit down and face you. If it is their first visit, ask, "Why are you here?" but do not invite a long story—you can usually get the information you need from the person's voice and body language, and of course the feedback from the instruments. Initial chitchat is really to help them to settle into the session and help you settle into the witnessing mode. Ask if they have any special concerns or conditions you should be aware of. Then take some time to create an affirmation for the session with them. You will learn how to do this in the next chapter.

A Word About Your Working Surface

Much sound healing work is done on a floor mat. On a single flat surface, the bowls resonate well and their vibrations can be felt through the floorboards. However, because of flexibility issues, age, or back problems, some practitioners work on a table. Many massage tables have accessories: attachable side wings with enough room to place the bowls in the hands and around the ankles and feet. Working on a massage table allows you to place bowls and gemstones underneath the table to work in additional dimensions, which is great. But because space is limited on a table, you will also need to bring in other work surfaces, and you should know that this will disrupt the resonance you can achieve on a single surface.

You will need to be creative when people can't get onto a table or on the floor because of serious physical challenges. As you learn to work with the directions (clockwise, counterclockwise, up, down) and as you get into the more advanced work, you will be able to adapt how you do your work to whatever physical constraints present themselves.

Practice Presencing

Once the person is settled in the space you have configured for the session, and is lying on the mat, invite them to take a few deep breaths to bring them into the present moment. Ask if it is okay to touch them during the session. (*Note:* Be sure you understand any limitations on touching that may be specific to the state where you are located.)

Now shift your attention to presencing. This is one of the simplest and most effective ways to set the stage for an effective session with the instruments. Presencing is the art of being available as a witness to the client—without judgment or an agenda. Even if you do nothing more than be an attentive witness, that by itself will be quite healing for your practice partner.

To practice presencing, first observe the person in their "normal" state so you can recognize the shifts that occur during a sound healing session. You can try this first with a friend:

- Ask them to lie down and close their eyes. Let them know that this is a silent practice—no talking.
- Observe *where their breath is situated.* Is it in the chest, abdomen, or rib cage? Somewhere else?
- Pay attention to the *rate of their breath.* Is it slow, fast, even, choppy?
- Now *scan their body* and note areas of tension. Are their eyelids fluttering or quiet? Is their face taut? Are their shoulders tense or relaxed? Look for twitches. Are they squirming a lot?
- Do nothing else—just observe.

You may be thinking that so far you haven't really *done* anything. Actually, you have already done a lot. Through silent observation, you have started the healing process by creating the space in which it can take place.

Note Your Observations

What did you observe? What thoughts, perceptions, or images came up for you? How comfortable were you with this silent observation? I recommend you create a form like the following and make notes after the session. Also ask your practice partner if they have any questions or feedback for you, and note anything of interest there as well. If you take our advanced training course, you will keep detailed logs on all your practice partners—a good habit to get into and essential for meeting your responsibility to maintain good records.

Name	Date	Observations	Practice Partner Feedback

Don't be surprised if you are not entirely comfortable during this silent observation: it is common for new practitioners to feel a little uneasy. But this is a vital part of creating the container for an effective session. During the few minutes it takes for the practitioner to center and observe, the practice partner or client has the opportunity to start relaxing into the space.

Your Turn

As is the case with many of the lessons in this book, you cannot absorb this one on presencing simply by reading. So before you read further, please find a few people to practice with. If this takes a little while to arrange, that's fine. It's worth it to take a break from the book and let your own experience teach you about presencing before you go any further. Be sure to use the form you created to note your own comfort level as well as what you see with your client.

Bring Your Practice Partner into the Healing Space with Touch

Now it's time to focus your attention on helping your practice partners access a quiet part of themselves. Sometimes people are so pumped up that they don't even realize how tense they are. Their minds are whirring out of control and they are far, far outside their bodies. Your job is to help them get in touch with where they really are and return them to the present moment. You can do this in a number of ways, depending on the modality you choose. I like the simplest of methods—laying on of hands—because in addition to being comforting, it signals to the body that something is about to happen and reminds the person that it is time to relax. (*Note:* When you are touching people, it should never be done with any pressure—you are gently placing your hands, not pushing your hands into any part of the person's anatomy.) You can help the quieting process along by placing an eye pillow over the eyes to create total darkness. Clients have told me that this simple technique helps reduce mind chatter.

As the person settles, you will see the body making involuntary movements, or hear the belly gurgle: all signs of releasing and discharging blocked energy. Soon after I begin a session, clients take a deep sigh—a sign of release of tension. Then their breathing becomes slow and regular. It shifts from their chest area to their lower abdominal region. Their closed eyelids cease their fluttering, a movement that usually indicates an active mind.

Occipital hold.

Begin by placing your hands under the occiput (the back of the head or skull) to engage the relaxation response. Hold this position for a minute or until the client gives a deep sigh. At this point I usually softly repeat the affirmations we have co-created (see Chapter 2).

Now invite your practice partner to take a few deep breaths, bringing the breath from feet to head, following the breath with their consciousness: up the torso into the neck, into the head—suspend it a moment, and then exhale through an open mouth exhalation on the sound of "ahhh" to *release* stress. Then they can take a few slow breaths in and out the nose to relax into themselves. This is also a simple way to engage your practice partners to take ownership. By doing breath work, they're taking part in the session rather than waiting for you to fix them.

By the way, you should include breath work in all your healing sessions. Doing some breath work yourself, and teaching your practice partner techniques to relieve stress, relax, and diminish pain through breath, will engage them and help them between sessions.

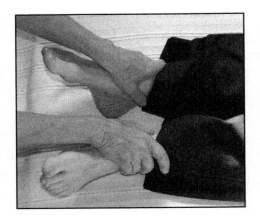 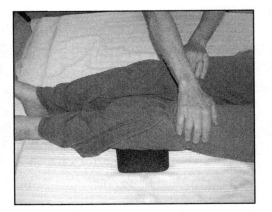

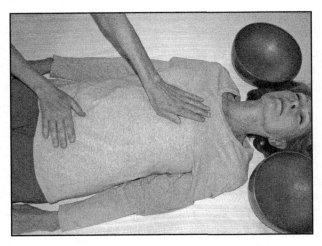

Presencing: ankles, knees, abdomen, and heart.

Now, gently releasing the head, place your hands on the client's shoulders and push down softly.

Next you will work your way up your client's body. The basic sequence is feet, ankles, knees, lower abdomen, solar plexus, heart, third eye, and crown chakra (the very top of the head—see the illustration of chakra locations on page 196). The entire process will take about five minutes.

Although this sequence seems quite simple, it is not as easy as it sounds and there are many things to pay attention to along the way. *Note:* As you travel around the body, make sure one hand always stays in contact as you move from one area to the next. This is important because it can be startling to feel both hands leaving the body at the same time.

Start by checking yourself. Close your eyes. Take a moment, a breath or two, and center yourself. Be comfortable with the silence.

- Making sure your hands are warm (if they aren't, rub them vigorously together until they are), place them on the client's ankles, gently and lightly without any pressure. Just allow them to be there and keep centered, with a steady breath. Watch the client for signs of relaxation such as a shift in breathing.
- Now place your hands on the client's knees, following the same instructions.
- Place your right hand in between your client's thighs, about a hand's length down the thigh and with the palm facing the root chakra. Place your left hand on their abdomen below the navel.
- Move your right hand to the abdomen below the navel and place your left hand on the heart.
- Move your right hand to the heart and place your left hand on the throat.
- Now place your right hand on the throat and the index finger of the left hand on the third eye, barely touching it.
- Finally, put the index finger of your right hand on the third eye and your left hand on the crown chakra.

A chakra is an energy center in the body. We will refer to seven of them in this book. Starting from the bottom, these are their names and associated colors: root chakra (red), sacral chakra (orange), solar plexus chakra (yellow), heart chakra (green), throat chakra (blue), third eye chakra purple), and crown chakra (white).

Your Turn

You will need to practice this technique at least twenty times before you really start to get the hang of it. During this time, make sure you have no other agenda besides presencing and observing your client. That is all you are doing—and it is exactly what is needed. As you refine this technique, you will be amazed at just how much comfort and shifting this alone will create in your client.

Working with Sound

Now it is time to bring sound into the session and work with the instruments. You will start with a diagnostic step, using the tingshas to locate imbalances and blocks, and then use the combination of other instruments that feels appropriate for shifting energy in a healing direction. You will learn these techniques in the chapters of Part II. For now, we'll skip over it and head toward the close of the session.

A Word About Detoxifying

A session with the bowls initiates the healing process, and a physical, emotional, and spiritual detoxification often occurs. Symptoms may include headache, nausea, and extremities feeling very hot or very cold. Some clients weep, and some tremble. When these symptoms occur it is time to reassure your client, help them breathe through their process, and make sure they drink plenty of water afterward. Although it can be most uncomfortable, detoxification is a good thing. Encourage clients to eliminate foods such as sugar, caffeine, alcohol, and refined wheat products from their diets and eat more fresh fruits and vegetables. This will greatly enhance the detoxification process. They can work with a nutritionist as well.

Closing a Session

At the end of the session, your practice partner will need a few minutes to regroup. You can simply sit there holding the space until they do. If they have fallen asleep, gently invite them to move their fingers and toes and slowly open their eyes. Then invite them to sit up. I suggest you remain silent and wait for them to speak. If they have questions, respond. Then offer them room-temperature water and remind them to drink plenty of water during the day.

Also suggest they take a nap after the first session if they are tired because a lot of release will have happened. In some cases—and especially after the first few sessions—relinquishing stored stress can feel exhausting. Some people respond to this feeling by forcing another adrenaline rush, perhaps by drinking coffee or eating something sugary, which keeps them in the same stress cycle. But for most of us, after we have experienced a strong release from stress and a reconnection to the universal flow and the feeling of being "home again," it's harder to make choices that take us away from this feeling of well-being. This is when the shifts occur that help us maintain our health, our sense of well-being, and our connection with "home."

After you have offered the person advice on caring for themselves, you can schedule the next session.

The Session at a Glance

Following is a summary of the typical flow of a session. Some of these steps may not be familiar to you yet, but you will learn much more about them in Parts II and III. I suggest you print out an enlarged copy of this page to use as a guide until you are comfortable with the flow of the session.

Remember: A session is not just about bowl layouts. It is the entirety of what happens during the time you and your practice partner are together.

1. Make sure all your instruments are where you need them, including pads (these are shelf liners cut to fit under the bowls so they don't move when struck or sun) and mallets.
2. Centering and raising your vibration (before practice partner arrives).
3. Greeting your practice partner and setting an intention/affirmation (coming into the present moment).
4. Relaxation head hold; breath work.
5. Presencing; hands-on work (feet to head, keeping contact with the body, connecting both of you).*
6. Tingshas diagnosis (strike three times first); use chart to notate changes in sound, moving at a slow pace and a consistent distance from body—see Appendix D for the chart. Then go back and work on those areas with the ganta and dorje.
7. Initial ganta/dorje work. Remember: clanking breaks up energy, singing soothes, and striking is great when using the infinity pattern or for gentle breaking up. Also, pay attention to the direction you work in. Working up is energizing and strengthening; working down is grounding and calming.
8. Foundational bowl layouts—striking and singing the bowls. If a bowl is out of tune or sounds strange, *stop* and fix it by using a ganta, singing, or creating a triad around it.

---

* If you are not authorized to touch a client, you can do this work etherically (without touching, using your intention), just above the body. But as a student doing practice sessions, you need not worry about this.

Head triad

Ankle triad

Hand-heart triad

Down the chakras—striking and singing to ground. Go up the chakras too if an increase in energy is needed, but always ground energy first.

Circling the body—singing a bowl (pay attention to which direction you travel)

Figure eight (can be done with a bowl or a ganta, depending on your intention)

Closing moves: head triad, grounding bowl (striking inward), and tingshas

Elements to remember: direction energy is being sent, harmony, blending of sounds, triads, volume and rhythm, texture of striking bowls on body, use of fire (middle) finger or air (index) finger, smooth, consistent singing of bowls, flow of the session (what to use, when, and how to use it, confidence in your own intuition, understanding of the energetic principle of each instrument)

This concludes our section on fundamentals. Next, in Part II, it's time to learn about the sacred healing instruments and how to get started using them!

Part II

The Sacred Sound Family:
The Instruments and How to Use Them

Life is a song, it has its own rhythm and harmony. It is a symphony of all things which exist, in major and minor keys of Polarity. It blends the discords, by opposites, into a harmony which unites the Whole into a symphony.

Miriam O'Mahony

Now I am going to introduce you to the family of sacred sound instruments. Some people (including me) sometimes refer to them as Tibetan instruments or bowls, but they are really Himalayan, coming from different countries along the mountain range including Nepal, Tibet, and the borders of Bhutan. They are highly symbolic and are also known as teachers of the dharma.

The symbolism and wonderful dharma stories associated with the shapes, designs, and uses of these instruments are mysterious and fascinating. It is very helpful to know this background information because the instruments are impregnated with the energy of the symbols and spiritual teachings. Here, however, we will focus more on the practical applications.

There are four instruments in the vibrational sound family that I use for healing, two of which, the ganta and dorje, are used together. In this section I devote chapters to each of them, followed by a chapter on bowl layouts and sacred geometry. Let's start with instruments that are used for diagnosis: the tingshas.

Chapter 4
THE TINGSHAS

Practitioner and temple tingshas.

Mantras inside tingshas.

Awaken and gather at attention. Something vital is about to occur. A healing, a blessing, a transformation. We, the tingshas, initiate the energy of the Three Jewels (in Tibetan Buddhism): the sanga (community) from the crown chakra, truth from the throat chakra, and compassion from the heart chakra. All entities of darkness, all bearers of fear—be welcome in our circle. Our energy is here to awaken the light within you through community, truth, and compassion. We exist to initiate the healing process, so wake up. Wake up now. For healing is a spiritual awakening that has a great impact on the physical body.

Look at these instruments. The two metal shapes connected by a leather string are reminiscent of little flying saucers, aren't they? And in a way, they are about space travel, as you shall soon see! In the Himalayas, tingshas are used in a variety of monastic rituals and ceremonies. They are made of a sacred twelve-metal alloy and will not break, so don't be afraid to strike them, but learn to be subtle too. They come in a variety of sizes and are often decorated with symbols, inside and out, and each one has its own distinct pitch.

Pictured on page 49 are practitioner and temple tingshas. The mantras on the insides of the tingshas represent what is known in Tibetan Buddhism as the "Three Jewels." These are three energies that are awakened in us when we strike the tingshas: the sanga, representing a gathering of people, normally for a spiritual cause (crown chakra); truth (throat chakra); and compassion (heart chakra).

In vibrational healing, tingshas are used:

- To clear the space before and after a session
- To signal or initiate the beginning of a healing session
- As a diagnostic tool using sound to locate energetic blocks or weaknesses in your client's body

How to Hold and Play the Tingshas

The following is the traditional way to hold and play the tingshas:

- Hold the leather string between your index fingers and thumbs close to the tingshas. Be careful not to put your fingers *on* the tingshas or you will retard the sound. This may feel strange to you at first, but you will get used to it.
- Hold the string firmly so the tingshas don't flop around.
- Briskly and firmly tap them together at right angles three times, and in sets of three. Pause a moment between each set and listen to the full ringing of the sound.
- At the very start of a session, after you have completed a set of three taps, you may hold one disc to your heart and the other facing toward your client. This projects your heart energy to your client.

Tingshas Diagnosis

Note: Please read these instructions entirely before you start.

I mentioned earlier that you can use the tingshas to help diagnose energetic or physical blockages, breaks, or areas of weakness. This requires a very well trained ear and many hours of practice. It is not easy to hear the nuances, and requires patience to learn.

Take plenty of time to practice striking the instruments, listening to the subtleties of their ring and vibration, and using your intention to direct their energy. Notice the difference in the texture of a room before and after you use them. Observe their effects on other people. Pay attention to changes in temperature in yourself and in your surroundings. Tingshas, like the other instruments, have different pitches. Select one you find pleasant that awakens your senses without overpowering you.

- Bring the tingshas near your ear and strike once sharply. Listen to the quality and texture of the sound. Listen to how the sound waves diminish and at what rate. Notice the quality of sound waves: for example, short, long, or vibrating. Hearing the variety of sound at this juncture gives you a baseline from which to conduct the diagnosis. (You may have to do this several times to establish a baseline.)

- Print out Tingsha Chart from Appendix D on page 246 so you can mark any fluctuations you hear as you go along. Fluctuations may include *fluttering, long waves,* or *deadening* of sound. It is helpful to create a symbol for each of these three sound textures.
- Now, starting at your practice partner's head, strike the tingshas. Slowly and steadily scan the body, holding one side of the instrument about two inches above the client and the other facing you so you can hear the fluctuations in sound. Move down one side of the body and then the other, listening for any variation of sound and striking the tingshas from time to time.
- The movement of this diagnosis is slow and steady. Although it will be your inclination (especially at first), *do not* go over the same spot again and again. This breaks continuity and the energy will shift somewhat compared to the first pass over the body. Beginners tend to go over a spot repeatedly because they don't trust what they hear or even *whether* they hear something at all. It is best to simply trust the first inclination. Also be very careful not to strike the tingshas too hard around the client's head and ears or it will become unpleasant for them.
- Keep the client-centered half of the tingshas at that two-inch point above the body at all times and move the other one, along with your body, toward it to strike it. Otherwise you will constantly be moving both arms up and down, again losing continuity.
- Mark fluctuations as you hear them on your stick-figure chart.

These fluctuations give you a good sense of where energy is blocked or overactive. In general, smooth, sustained sound waves signify that energy is running smoothly in that region. Fluttering can mean a "hot spot." Sometimes the sound flutters over the third eye, signifying that it is active. If there is strong fluttering over a joint or muscle, it may mean overactivity in that area (for example, a wrist affected by too much computer work). The sound of the tingshas will deaden markedly where there has been surgery, a break, or a region of the body that needs energy or awakening. You can work with gantas and/or bowls on those regions (see Chapters 5 and 6). Long waves are an indication of harmonious flow of energy. The sound is quite subtle with tingshas and can often be felt rather than heard directly. When you strike the tingshas, be aware of how you sense the long wave— through your ears or entire body.

A good metaphor for the tingshas is that using them is like putting the key in the ignition of a car and starting it. They awaken and initiate healing. We'll get back to the tingshas later. Now let's move on to the other sacred sound instruments.

Chapter 5
THE GANTA AND DORJE (OR VAJRA)

Ganta (bell) and Dorje (scepter).

We officiate the dance of Divine Feminine and masculine within you. We sow the seeds of wisdom and compassion, moving our energies through your body into your every thought, word, and deed.

The ganta (bell) and dorje (scepter) represent, respectively, the sacred female and male aspects of our beings. To be balanced ourselves, we need to acknowledge the attributes of each and balance their energies within us. These important instruments are used by Tibetan monks in ceremonies and rituals in Nepal or Tibet. They are like two sides of a coin, interdependent parts of the whole. Although they have a highly mystical aspect, they are also used on a practical level in vibrational healing. They move energy. To go back to the car analogy again, using the ganta and dorje is like putting the car into gear and giving it some gas.

In the Buddhist tradition, the ganta is symbolic of the body, the dorje of the mind, and the sound of the bell is regarded as the *speech of the Buddha*. Traditionally, the ganta and dorje were used to call people to practice while warding off malevolent energies. They're still used as calling instruments in monastic ceremonies, often done in a cross-handed position. That is, the hands are crossed over the heart, with the ganta in the left hand and the dorje in the right. Then both hands move from the heart toward the ground as the left hand clacks the ganta.

Let's look a little more deeply at each of these instruments.

The Ganta

The ganta, or bell, is regarded as the universal symbol of wisdom or female energy and is always held in the left hand. This is because energy is received via our feminine or left side. The energy of feminine wisdom is moved by clacking or singing the bell to shift energy powerfully or gently. Traditionally, it is rung with a definitive, patterned rhythm.

The sound of the ganta is strong and can be piercing, and it can emit a variety of tones from low to high. Like the bowls, it can be sung in a clockwise or counterclockwise direction. In the Tibetan Buddhist tradition, anything that moves in a clockwise direction sends energy, prayers, or blessings outward; moving counterclockwise gathers energy inward. This is an important principle to learn—you will use it often.

In vibrational healing the ganta is used as an invocation to practice and to break up or move constricted energy. In her dynamic way, the ganta dissipates areas of dark or stuck energy like a laser. The ganta is useful in working with depression, tumors, growths, and fears, among other things. I might use the ganta if someone has acute back pain or an infection.

Like the bowls, gantas come in several sizes and in a range of qualities.

Singing the ganta.

The photograph on page 54 shows two ganta/dorje sets, one that has been dipped in silver and one with a gold-dipped handle and dorje. The craftsmanship of both is of higher quality than regular practitioner gantas, and the gold handled type is the highest quality, both in terms of craftsmanship and sound. Note that since these instruments are handmade, they have irregularities. For example, the string holding the clacker may be too long or too short, making it difficult to clack in a steady rhythmic pattern. In that case, simply adjust the length by either cutting or replacing it so that it works for you.

Gantas are calibrated to specific regions of the body. In the Tibetan tradition, there are three general regions: lower (root/sacral), middle (torso), and upper (third eye/crown). Gantas have either flower petals or stars inscribed inside them (though some are hard to see). The fewer the petals, the lower the region of the body the ganta is best used for (for example, a four-to-six-petal instrument is geared to the lower, root/sacral area; eight to twelve petals indicate the mid-range, solar plexus/throat; and more than that is appropriate for the upper range, third eye/crown). If your ganta has stars within it, the five-pointed star is geared to the third eye and the six-pointed star is appropriate for the heart chakra. Most practitioners have at least one ganta to use for each region of the body. If you can see the petals or the star pattern inside the ganta, that is ideal, but if you don't, use your intuition coupled with your intention to determine which regions of the body to use it with.

Eight-petal lotus inside ganta.

Striking and Singing the Ganta

It's important to gain mastery in creating the different voices of the ganta so you can direct them to where they will be the most effective. When people first get a ganta and start clacking it, it can sound so loud and horrible that they want to run out of the room. But you can clack a ganta in a way that breaks up energy gently. It's really very rare that somebody is made out of wrought iron and you need to come down on them with a sledgehammer. So, please don't use the ganta as a sledgehammer! Practice until you can clack softly and gently.

When you hold the ganta, make sure to grasp the upper part of the shaft so your hand doesn't retard the sound by touching the bell itself. Create a steady rhythm by flicking your wrist in one direction only. Or you can flick it back and forth, making sure to create a clear pattern. Also, pay attention to the face of the female deity (bodhisattva) on the shaft of the ganta. When you want to direct energy outward, turn her face outward, away from you; when you want to bring energy inward, direct her face toward you. With practice, you can create a clean, distinct sound.

Textures and Volume

Each of the instruments you're working with has many different textures. Each texture has a specific task and usage. Listen to them and see how you respond to those sounds, because someone else is probably going to have a similar reaction. Spend a lot of time singing that ganta until you can really feel where the edge is and can create just one beautiful, consistent sound for several minutes.

Then practice with your wrists to move the clacker until you can get whatever rhythm you choose. Practice until you can play the breaking-up pattern so softly that you can barely hear it. Then start bringing up the volume, and then bring the volume down again, until you're very practiced at increasing and decreasing the volume when you use the clacker.

The Voices of the Ganta

Remember that the ganta has many voices with which it can break up energy, and it takes quite a bit of practice to create gentle rhythmic patterns as the clacker strikes the side of the instrument. Patterns can include three, six, or more clacks, but remember that the sound needs to be consistent, not haphazard, and *gentle*.

When you are learning to clack the ganta, try creating a rhythmic pattern of three clacks one after the other. Now try the same pattern but allow five seconds between clacks. You will see that one pattern is energizing and the other is calming. Practice clacking the ganta so quietly that the sound is barely noticeable, increasing in volume until it is loud, then decreasing again. Getting accustomed to this will allow you to control how much volume you project in any given situation. If it is uncontrolled, the sound can be startling to a person who is deeply relaxed.

Always use the padded side of a stick to *strike* and the bare wooden part of it to *sing* a ganta. To powerfully enhance energy, you can strike the ganta using rhythmic patterns. By contrast, singing the ganta is soothing and releasing if sung clockwise, and soothing and nourishing if sung counterclockwise.

When you have completed your tingshas body scan, strike or sing the ganta above the regions of the body you have determined need their help. For example, if your tingshas diagnosis indicated fluttering and you have already broken up, dispersed, and grounded that energy, singing the ganta in a clockwise direction would be appropriate to soothe that area—calming it down. If the tingshas diagnosis indicated a swallowing of sound and lack of energy, then after the initial breaking up and grounding, counterclockwise singing would help nourish and reawaken the area. You could follow this with some rhythmic tapping with the stick to energize. Any one of these methods is appropriate, depending on the texture of sound that will most effectively address the issue at hand.

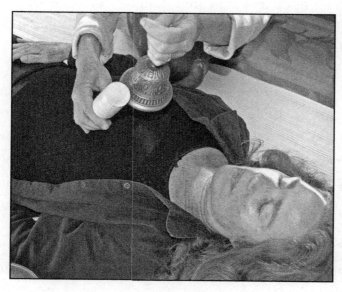

Singing the ganta.

If someone has a tumor or a gallstone, is struggling with a lot of anger that needs to be broken up, or has some really sluggish earth energy, breaking up the energy by clacking is a good idea—but never too vigorously because the clacking voice can easily become too harsh. It is rarely necessary to clack loudly, and doing so can bring a client out of a relaxed state or even frighten them. It's best to start with a *very quiet volume* and work up to a little louder using a rhythmic pattern (for example, clacking three or six times quietly, pausing, and repeating that pattern several more times, increasing the volume each time).

As I mentioned, striking the ganta with the padded stick is invigorating, and you can do it using single strikes or in a pattern that includes sacred geometry (see the section beginning on page 83). Singing the ganta is soothing and nurturing. The best way for you to understand the nuances is to first sing a ganta, starting off very, very quietly and then singing it louder and louder and louder. This way you will hear how powerful it is in terms of moving energy, but also how sweet and comforting it is. Then you can adjust the volume when singing it to suit the situation you are working with. Sometimes you need gentle and soothing, and sometimes you need gentle with a bit more power behind it. Make sure that when you sing the ganta, as with the bowls, you keep the sound consistent and beautiful to create a feeling of safety.

Each of these voices calls forth an aspect of wisdom, and it is important to match the texture of the sound you create with the issue at hand. It is also nice to sing the ganta and end with a strike as punctuation.

You can also use the ganta to motivate the energy of an intention or affirmation in a healing session. For example, you might want to say the affirmation and then use the ganta to move it through the space and through the person's body.

More Ways to Use the Ganta

There are many ganta techniques for clearing the chakras. If someone is depleted physically or energetically, you can place crystals on a depleted chakra and gently ring (clack) the ganta over the chakra to break up stuck energy. Then you can clear and spin the chakra using the dorje. You can use metal dorjes on and around the body, but crystal dorjes are great for clearing because they are crystalline, like the inside of our bones, and because of their amplification qualities. Crystal dorjes are handmade and come in a variety of sizes from tiny (to be used on the third eye) to quite large. Refer to the Resources section on page 248 for more.

You will also use the ganta to help bring up the voice of a bowl, to awaken it, or to bring it into harmony. Make sure to hold it so that it is positioned inside the bowl and strike it, and then bring it up to about a foot above the bowl, striking it and then the bowl until they are in harmony with each other. Then strike the bowl and the bowls around it to make sure it is in harmony with them.

1.   2.   3.

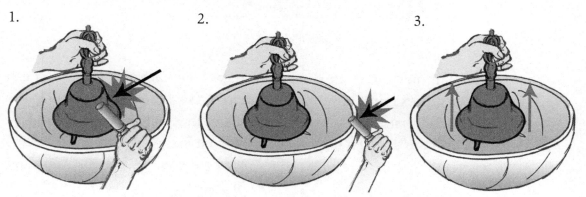

1. Bell in bowl, striking bell. 2. Bell in bowl, striking edge of bowl. 3. Bell in bowl, with bell and bowl sounds interacting.

Another option for using the ganta is to work the long lines of the body (see the diagram on page 62). I learned about long lines as part of my training in polarity therapy and energy balancing and have found they are easily integrated into sound healing. In fact, the sacred sound instruments are wonderful for integrating with other modalities that you already use.

If you trace the center line of your body, starting from the center line of your head and then traveling down in between your two collar bones, you'll find a little space, a little V notch that you can feel with your fingers. Follow that center line all the way down the central core of your body past your root chakra. This is the ether line. In terms of polarity, the ether line is neither positive nor negative; it is neutral.

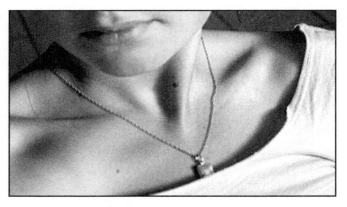

Collar bones. Photo: Juli Zib

You can move from this neutral (ether) core, working from the head down. As an example, you might sing or strike the ganta and move the energy from that central ether line down the body, maybe to reduce hypertension or anxiety. If someone is agitated, has a lot of anger, or seems to be nervous or anxious, you want to disperse and ground that energy.

Notice in the diagram that on each side of the ether line are additional long lines corresponding to the elements: air, fire, water, and finally earth. If you use the collarbone to locate these elemental lines, they start about an inch out from the ether line on both sides of the body, with the earth line being on the outermost edge. You can ring or sing the ganta and sweep over these long lines from top to bottom, or vice versa, on one side and then the other side. Avoid going too fast.

In addition to the ether line, you can work with whatever line most

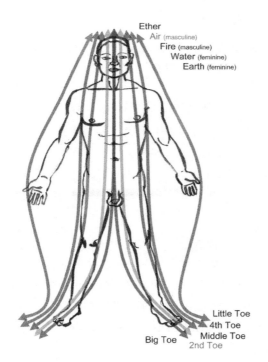

Elemental long lines.

fits the situation. If the person is angry you would ground the fire line and then energize the water line. If they are confused, or overly active mentally, you can ground the air line and energize the earth line and follow this with a figure eight over the entire body to balance. You can also make a figure-eight pattern over an area to create connection and expand that balancing to the rest of the body. Sweep from the feet to the head over the earth and water lines if your client is suffering from low blood pressure or depression, is tired with low energy, or lacks creative energy. Another option is to sweep down and then up the body. This smooths out the emotional layer of the aura.

For more on polarity, see Chapter 8.

Using the Ganta to Release Stuck Energy in the Joints

Energy often gets stuck in the joints of the body. You can often hear this during the tingshas diagnostic as the tingshas get louder or seem to flutter more over the joints.

Use your creative intuition along with the basic principles. If you use a ganta on the joints where there has been overactivity, you can gently use the clacker to break up the energy in the joints, then ground that energy into the earth, and then sing in a clockwise direction to soothe and release. If the joints are dull and you hear a deadening sound with the tingshas, you might ground the stuckness first, then strike the ganta in a rhythmic pattern to energize, and then make a spiraling circle counterclockwise to reawaken and nourish the energy in that area.

Since this work is always about energy balancing, to release inflammation in areas of pain or swelling, you can work with the masculine and the feminine energies by placing the dorje (masculine) on a certain joint after the initial clearing, and then do a clockwise spiral around the joint with the ganta (feminine).

Always keep in mind the principles of using these instruments as you work. Maybe the joints are just fine and they don't need to be cleared. Maybe during your tingshas diagnostic you pass over a joint and the tingshas sound drops or deadens. What is that telling you? That there's very little energy moving, and that the joint needs counterclockwise work to reawaken and bring in energy after first releasing and grounding what may be stuck there. If the tingshas go crazy with very fast vibrations, they're telling you that there's too much energy. This part of the body is like a hot spot.

Pay attention to what the sounds of the instruments are telling you and then think about the best way to work with that while practicing the basic principles of moving energy. After a while this will become second nature. So for example, if during a tingshas diagnostic (or at any other time) you notice that the energy in the knee is stuck and dead, what kind of a texture of sound would you use? Would you want to break up energy, soothe, or energize? Maybe a combination of textures would be best.

What if during the course of your session you feel you've found a hot spot? Perhaps the area is swollen or has a rash. What do you do? What does a hot spot need? You don't want to give it more energy. The first thing you want to do is to clear and soothe it very gently, moving the ganta clockwise. Then you might do a figure eight to balance it even more.

The Dorje or Vajra

Although it is part of the family of sacred sound instruments, you may be surprised to learn that the dorje does not make a sound. Instead, it is the representation of pure energy, a radiant and indestructible symbol of the transcendental state of emptiness and the masculine aspect of compassion, associated with the right side of our body. He is always presented as the counterpart to his sister, the ganta, and held in the right hand or placed to the right of the ganta. He too moves energy, not through sound but via placement and intention.

Dorje on chest.

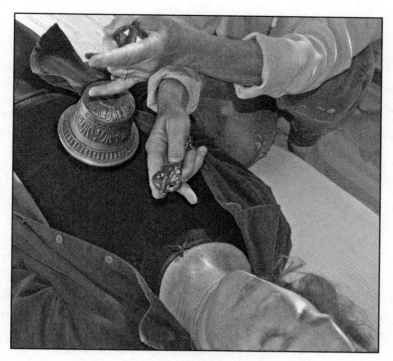

Using the ganta and dorje together.

Also known by the Tibetan name *vajra*, the dorje is made up of several parts and represents the divine masculine. In the very center of the dorje is a sphere that represents oneness, the primordial nature of the universe, the underlying unity of all things: nonduality.

Emerging from the sphere are two eight-petaled lotus flowers. One represents the phenomenal world, or in Buddhist terms, *samsara*—physicality, the material world, the mundane. The other side represents *nirvana*, the spiritual and etheric world. Together they represent one of the fundamental dichotomies perceived by the so-called unenlightened.

The basic precept of all suffering, according to Tibetan Buddhism, is the illusion that we are separate. The sphere in the center of the dorje removes this separation, joining the physical with the spiritual at the central sphere

Around the mouth of the lotus petal are mythical creatures that appear to be half fish and half crocodile. These creatures were made up of several animals that represent the union of opposites: harmonization of qualities that transcend our usual experience. The spiritual, mythical, and phenomenal are all part of the Tibetan Buddhist tradition.

Most dorjes have five prongs and a central shaft that goes through them. There's a system of correspondences between these elements of the phenomenal and the spiritual.

The dorje is used in a couple of ways within the context of vibrational healing:

- To focus energy on a specific area
- To direct energy from one point to the other

Ways to Use the Dorje

In terms of practical use, you can place the dorje directly on the body, connecting areas that are challenged with those that are healthy and directing energy from one to the other. If one ovary is challenged and the other one is healthy, for instance, you can place a dorje between them and use intention to move the energy from the healthy one to strengthen the weaker one. If you're having an issue concerning masculine and feminine, you might want to put it in a horizontal fashion across the body to help equalize the masculine and feminine aspects. You can also place the central sphere of the dorje on a specific area of the body to direct and amplify energy to that location. To magnify that energy, use a crystal dorje (one quality of crystal being that it amplifies energy).

If a person's heart is open but they are experiencing difficulty communicating, I might place the dorje vertically between the heart and the throat. Or if they are holding on to sadness in their second chakra, I might place it vertically between that chakra and the heart.

The other way to use the dorje is to hold it in your hand like a pointer to move energy up, down, around, and through the body. You can think of it almost like using an etheric Etch-a-Sketch. If I wish to align the chakras from head to foot, I might use it as a pointer while I direct my intention to clearing and aligning the energetic centers. I can also hold the dorje with intention while playing the ganta. (Many more techniques are available in our introductory workshop materials: see Further Resources.)

Get the idea? Of course, all of this needs to be done with intention and focus.

Tracing the Line of Kundalini

If you understand the principles of moving energy with the sacred sound tools, you may take some intuitive, creative liberties. One pattern is to use the ganta and dorje together at the very end of the session to trace the line of the flow of *kundalini*. Kundalini is the energy of Creation that resides in the root chakra and can rise up through the other chakras of the body.

Only do this technique at the very end of a session with clients whose energy has been cleared and aligned to establish a clear path between the root chakra and the crown chakra—and beyond. Imagine a tube going from your root chakra all the way up the spine. Now picture a fire—very powerful energy—at the bottom of the tube. It's easy to see that the tube would need to be clear and unobstructed to accommodate the rising of that very powerful energy all the way up the kundalini channel. If it's not, as the movement of energy encounters energy constrictions, it can create something like an explosion. You don't want that to happen!

To move kundalini energy up the central channel, take the ganta in your left hand and the dorje in your right hand. Begin at the root chakra and make two S shapes as you travel up the body, basically at the same time. (You might have seen this pattern in medical journals or medical logos—the image of the caduceus, two snakes twisting up a shaft.) Your hands will start beside one another at the root and then you will cross and uncross them, making two S patterns as you work around each chakra and up the body.

Reviewing What You Have Learned: Practice Time

So far you have learned some preliminary aspects of using these instruments. There is much more to it, but by now you have already gained knowledge of some the foundational aspects. To continue your practice of the preliminaries, ask a friend to work with you. Explain that this is a practice session and that you will ask them for feedback afterward. Then take these steps:

- Prior to their arrival, practice clearing and grounding yourself.
- Create a calm, peaceful environment to welcome your friend into.
- Place a mat and blanket on the floor for them to lie on.
- Make sure the room is warm enough.
- When they arrive, create an affirmation with them for both of you to hold during the session.
- Invite them to lie on the mat and explain that they will feel you touching them gently. Invite them to let you know if they experience any discomfort.
- Place yourself at the crown of their head and spend a few moments observing only. Then, with your hands under their occipital bone, invite them to take a few slow, deep breaths and practice presencing until you are ready to begin the hands-on portion of the session.
- Strike the tingshas to open the session and conduct a body scan making notes on a body image chart on what you hear as you scan each section of the body.
- Go to their feet and conduct the hands-on part of the session as described beginning on page 40.
- Be careful to note any body language, shifts in energy, or movement.
- Practice using the ganta to move stuck energy or further open/ enliven an area.
- Now allow your client a few moments to regroup. Invite them to sit up.
- Offer them something to drink and ask them to describe how the session felt to them and what they noticed.
- As they are commenting, graciously accept everything they say, making mental notes.

Conduct these practice sessions many times, until you are very comfortable with this process, before moving on. Keep good notes to document your progress and your partner's remarks from session to session.

Chapter 6
THE SINGING BOWLS

Singing bowls stacked.

Bowls have been used in many cultures dating back hundreds of years to pre-shamanic periods. The ancient bowls we are discussing here originated in several areas in the Himalayas, hence are called Himalayan bowls. But they are also known as Tibetan bowls, and the terms are often used interchangeably. They come in a variety of shapes and sizes and have different markings on them depending on the region where they were made. You will read more about this in a bit.

The ancient Himalayan bowls are made from a consecrated seven-metal alloy that, when skillfully stimulated, produces at least five individual and simultaneous tones, each at its own consistent high frequency, which vibrationally dance with each other, creating overtone upon overtone of delightful harmonics. As you may recall, high-frequency vibrational sound is the most effective for healing.

Strike your bowl. Listen. How many tones can you hear? Most people can hear three, but many can hear a few more too. Because of the harmonics, no two bowls are the same and although there is a fundamental note, the pitch will change depending on how and where you strike the bowl and what kind of striker you use. If you strike two bowls at the same time, they will harmonize with one another and the pitch may change yet again! However, if you keep the other variables constant, it is possible to approximate the fundamental pitch of a bowl by using a digital tuner.

I don't assign much importance to knowing the exact *note* of a bowl because I am more interested in *tones* and how they harmonize with each of the other bowls in my collection. Different tones and harmonics will come up as I play the bowls for different people and that is also of greater interest to me.

Other aspects that are important in bowl sound include the *flavor* of the sound. Is it warm and grounding or high and energizing? Is it a well-balanced bowl, with both warm and high qualities? Does the sound stay constant for a long time or does it lose volume quickly? Pay attention to all these things.

The raw materials used in the best of these bowls were said to be collected, smelted, purified, cast, reheated, and hammered into shape and tone by Himalayan monks who devoted their lives to spiritual practice. They recited mantras or sacred chants while making the bowls and infused this intent into the instruments. Their sound synchronizes brain waves and creates a therapeutic effect that brings the physical frequencies of body and mind into alignment for mind/body realization. Following are the metals used, along with their planetary aspects and physical associations:

The Seven-Metal Alloy

> *Silver*—Moon; physical association: time, joy, instinct
>
> *Gold*—Sun; physical association: heart, spirit
>
> *Mercury*—Mercury; physical association: intellect, speech
>
> *Tin*—Jupiter; physical association: insight, wisdom
>
> *Lead*—Saturn; physical association: conscience, discipline
>
> *Copper*—Venus; physical association: love, art
>
> *Iron*—Mars; physical association: action, sexuality

For Tibetans, iron is of principle importance because of its sacred origins: meteorites found at the summits of the Himalayas. But as Dr. Jeffrey Thompson once explained in a workshop I attended, the iron in our blood is magnetized and moves through our bodies in the form of an electromagnetic field. Science tells us that water is a better conductor of information than air, so the sympathetic resonance of the iron in the bowl imparts a potent charge to the iron in our blood as it circulates through the system.

Earlier in this book we discussed the role of intention in effective healing. With this in mind, healers will want to use instruments whose very existence is rooted in the intention of healing and transformation. This is why ancient Himalayan bowls are greatly preferable to those created for commerce by modern means.

Richard Rudis describes the nature of the bowls beautifully in this passage:

> The Singing Bowls produce the primordial sound of "AUM": the fundamental utterance of energy metamorphosing into matter. They alter space, mind, and time, awakening cellular memory and healing the energy body. The act of listening to their captivating overtones effectively stops one's internal

dialogue, the "Monkey Mind." The individual is transported into a space of tranquility and balance where the "Universal Chord" found within each self is touched, joined with, and understood. The Universal Chord is the primordial substance from which our whole reality is made and from which our Universe originated. [2]

You will see that although the vibrations of the Himalayan bowls can be directed to a specific area of the body for healing purposes, they work on a more fundamental level, impacting the totality of body, mind, and spirit.

A Side Note: Crystal Bowls and Tuning Forks

As you have just learned, authentic Himalayan bowls are made of a special seven-metal alloy and work on a fundamental level with the whole-body concept of illness. Because of their harmonics and their having been imbued with blessings and prayers, they work on all levels, supporting the interconnectedness of all things and creating a harmonious alignment. Crystal bowls, like tuning forks, are calibrated to specific energy centers (chakras) or organs and thus are most effective when working with one specific part of the body and its function, more like a surgical scalpel. I prefer the Himalayan bowls because they balance and harmonize the entire energetic, spiritual, and physical system and because of the intention that goes into their making. I also much prefer the harmonics of the metal alloy bowls to the single tones of crystal bowls, but I do acknowledge they can successfully be used together.

What Are the Healing Benefits of the Bowls?

We use these instruments for meditation and physical vibrational healing. Their harmonic resonances have a wide array of remarkable healing effects. They:

- Reduce stress
- Balance the chakras to create dynamic centering

- Produce vitality synchronization, stabilizing energy/vitality and facilitating spontaneous healing
- Effectively alter consciousness into a peaceful and expansive meditative state (trance induction)
- Deepen meditation
- Engage the relaxation response
- Reduce brain activity and body temperature
- Inhibit pain
- Stabilize blood pressure
- Create clarity of mind
- Help shift perspective
- Promote overall well-being

People report a fundamental shift in their view of phenomena and space; accentuated clarity of mind and body; enhanced creativity, vigor, and joy; and sense of peace.

Types of Himalayan Bowls

There are several types of Himalayan bowls. The main ones I use are the Thadobadi (Bhutanese), Ramuna (Nepalese), and Manipuri and Jambati (Tibetan). Thadobadi bowls were created specifically for the purpose of physical healing, with the secondary effect being altered consciousness. You can see by their shape that sounds travel more directly down or up.

Tibetan bowls (Jambatis are large, Manipuris smaller) were mainly created for altering consciousness, with the secondary effect being physical healing. They are shaped in such a way that the sound is more expansive.

The end result with both types is the same: healing and transformation. Other kinds of bowls include Cobrabati, Ultrabati, Lingham, Yoni, and more. I have included photos of a couple of these, but for purposes of instruction, we will stick with the Thadobadi, Ramuna, Manipuri, and Jambati.

Tibetan Bowls

Tibetan bowls.

There are several types of Tibetan bowls: small ones known as Manipuri or heart bowls (front row), and medium- and large-sized bowls, known as Jambati (back row). Notice the graceful shape and the gentle rising of the chime from the base. In the Tibetan bowls, the base is much smaller than the opening and the chime is very rounded, with no edges. Note the various sizes. These bowls were made for the purpose of altering consciousness for hundreds of years prior to the Chinese invasion, when many were destroyed or hidden. Most of the ancient Tibetan bowls were made in monasteries along its eastern border. One such region produced the bowls that have numerous markings on them from the manner in which they were pounded into shape. They are called hor bowls (back left) and the dark hammer marks are clearly visible. The bowls are no longer produced in the same way. Some are still hand hammered but not in monasteries or by monks. Many are made on lathes and then made to look old. Most are made for the purpose of commerce and certainly no longer contain, gold, silver, or iron from meteorite deposits.

Thadobadi (Bhutanese) bowls.

In Bhutanese or thadobati bowls, the base is larger in proportion to the opening and the chime has an edge. The sides rise up in a straight rather than a rounded shape. They were made with the primary intention of physical healing.

Nepalese bowl.

The Ramuna (Nepalese bowl) is much lighter and thinner than the others, and the base, which is very small, has a dimple inside. The sides of the Nepalese bowl look a bit more pregnant than the others, as you can see.

Ultrabadi bowl.

Ultrabadi bowls have a protruding upper lip. They are large, lighter than Jambatis, and can have a lovely, deep sound. They are often placed below the feet for a grounding effect.

Yoni bowl.

Yoni bowls are very heavy and thick, and their sound is pure and resonant. They sound more like a chime with one strong penetrating note.

Sticks and Sound

A variety of sticks.

You can use a wide variety of sticks to play the bowls. This is because every stick produces a different quality or tone, depending on the type of wood, the thickness, and the density. Some sticks are covered with monks' robes, felt, or leather—you will see why momentarily.

You can strike a bowl or you can sing a bowl. Let's take a look at both.

Striking a Bowl

When I want to produce a deep, rich-sounding vibration, I use the long-handled gonger because it calls forth the base sounds of the bowls in a gentle way. I tend to strike the bowl close to the base to get this droning sound.

When I want to bring up more of the tones, including the higher tones, I use a robe- or felt-covered stick and strike on the edge like this:

Tap bowl with padded stick.

Depending on the density of the wood—and hardwood always produces a better sound—you will get variation in the sound, so it's great to have a nice variety.

You can also turn the bowl upside down on your fist and play it with a gong mallet or padded stick.

Using the bowl like a gong.

To create a resonance and send it down your inner core, try placing a large bowl on your head. Be sure that the edges are not touching any part of your head or hair. Hold the bowl in place with one finger and strike with the gong.

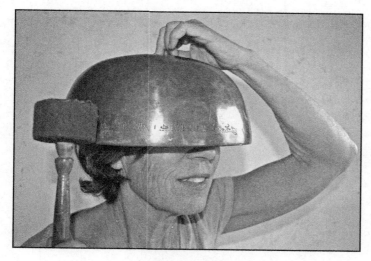

Bowl on head.

When you strike the bowl in your hand, you must never have your fingers on the body of the bowl; this will restrict the sound. People with long fingers often make the mistake of allowing their fingers to grasp the sides of the bowl. Hold your hand out flat and the bowl in your palm *or* hold the bowl up with your fingers.

Incorrect.

Correct.

Note: Never strike a bowl with bare wood. Always use the padded end of your stick. The bowls are metal but they can crack.

Singing a Bowl

Singing a bowl involves a different method altogether. To sing the bowl, you use the wooden part of a stick, with one exception: singing the bowl with a leather-covered stick brings out the lowest tones and more vibration.

Singing the bowl with a large wooden stick.

Begin by holding the stick in your hand like a pencil. Marry the stick to the edge of the bowl so it stands perpendicular to the bowl. Now, using your whole arm (not just your wrist), drag the stick around the outer rim of the bowl, staying connected with your breath. You can use pressure from your index finger on the stick to help maintain contact between the stick and the bowl. The movement should be slow and consistent, not fast and choppy. But you may find you're moving too slowly and need to speed up too!

Remember that the bowls are made of several metals, and it can take them a while to warm up. If you play your bowls for at least twenty minutes, the texture and quality of their sound will change markedly.

Your Turn

Now take a break from reading and practice singing your bowl.

One of three things may happen:

- You can't get any sound.
- You get a lot of screeching or choppy-sounding chatter.
- You get a great sound and love it!

It may surprise you to learn that not every bowl will sing for everyone. It is a mystery, but a bowl might sing for you and not for your friend. I think it has something to do with the chemistry between you and the bowl, the energy between you—everything is energy, remember? These instruments are great teachers, and if a bowl will not sing for you, you might ask yourself what you need to learn. It may be patience, perseverance, or letting go of control. It can be any number of things. The bowls will teach you if you let them.

Here are tips if your bowl is chattering: try slowing down, increasing the pressure of the stick against the bowl, and reversing direction. It isn't a bad idea to make friends with the chatter either, and allow it to be part of the experience.

If you couldn't get any sound, you might check a few things.

- Are you playing with the wooden or leather part of the stick?
- Is your stick the best weight and size for the bowl?
- Is there enough pressure between the edge of the bowl and the stick?
- Are you circling the bowl using your entire arm or just your wrist?
- Are you creating a consistent pattern of circling?
- Are you being patient enough?
- Are your fingers impeding the sound by being placed anywhere but on the very base of the bowl?

If you correct these things and the bowl still won't play, perhaps it is very, very old and simply needs to be played a great deal before it sings. It might be the wrong bowl for you and you need to find another one. More likely, the bowl is fine and you just need to be patient and consistent in playing it.

Spend a few hours to practice playing the bowls with a variety of sticks. Sing them, strike them, put them on your fist or on the floor. Establish a relationship with these wonderful instruments and experience the subtle sounds and vibrations they emit.

Chapter 7

Bowl Layouts and Sacred Geometry

Sacred geometry refers to the fundamental underlying patterns ("wave form language") of the material universe. These patterns bleed into our subconscious mind and reappear as symbols that we use to better understand ourselves, our nature, and our placement in universal being.[3]

Richard Rudis

This chapter was written in collaboration with Richard Rudis and covers the common bowl layouts you will use in your sound healing work. To help you gain an understanding of what's behind these configurations, let's start with *sacred geometry*.

On Sacred Geometry

Sacred geometry is a vast subject, and students of sound healing would do well to study it on their own; it can greatly enhance the effectiveness of your treatments. Here I offer some of the basic principles involved.

Sacred geometry is an ancient science that reveals how the energy patterns of Creation itself organize themselves in every natural pattern of life and growth through geometric shapes. These geometric patterns or codes, known as the blueprint of Creation, are intimately interconnected with our consciousness on a deeply spiritual level, yet we can recognize them every day in our environment: in ice crystals, snowflakes, DNA, pine cones, flower petals, and really all life forms. Working with these codes awakens in us the ability to rediscover the intrinsic balance, perfection, and harmony of every situation as well as our nondualistic connection to the universe.

Sacred geometry is also known as "divine proportion" and can be found in sacred architecture, art, and music. Going back thousands of years, these complex systems have been identified as part of the "great design": universally reoccurring patterns observed and identified in relationship to one another. Historical examples of this are found in Hindu and Buddhist mandalas, depictions of chakras, yantras, ancient Western labyrinths, religious Flowers of Life, and Tree of Life symbols.

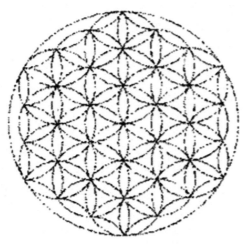

Flower of Life

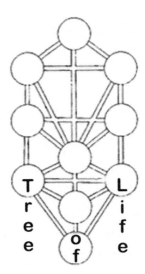

When we utilize patterns of sacred geometry in healing sessions, we awaken the corresponding energies in our clients. Knowing the symbolism and energies associated with a particular sacred geometry shape helps us utilize it effectively. There is a vast difference in effectiveness between being fully engaged with the pattern you use and superimposing patterns onto the bowls with too little understanding.

The first phase of understanding sacred geometry is to develop an intimate dialogue with it in yourself before you work with practice partners or clients, so as to fully awaken to its transformative power. Patterns include the pyramid, pentagon, six-pointed star, spiral, and more.

Exploring on Your Own

Here are some methods for working with and integrating sacred geometry into your life:

- Gaze at the patterns.
- Search for and identify the patterns in objects, nature, and art. When you notice a pattern, notice too what the quality of the pattern is and its effect on the environment.
- Draw the pattern repeatedly as you notice its energy within you.
- Create patterns with bowls on the floor and walk them, play them, and allow them to become an extension of self.
- Meditate on the forms.

Sacred Geometry in Sound Healing

Sound itself is a naturally repeating aspect of the physical universe. As such, it is embedded within sacred geometric expressions. Yet it is important to distinguish between music, which is an *intellectual construct*, and sound: *sacred geometry is not a construct of the mind*. The sound we make use of in sound healing is a naturally occurring phenomenon, an extension of the universe that influences us physically, emotionally, mentally, and spiritually.

We use sacred geometry in sound healing to produce a matrix of sound energy—you could think of it as an "envelope" in which healing takes place. These configurations create powerful harmonizing structures we can build upon, using our instruments to amplify the sacred geometry that is naturally found within the human body.

Four general states of consciousness can be affected in this way: physical, emotional, mental, and spiritual. If we imagine a state of good health as a room with four walls, each of these conscious states would be a doorway. We use sacred sound energy to modify one or more of these thresholds, resulting in profound changes in the body.

Three Important Shapes

Sacred geometry takes many forms, but here I will mention three of them and what they can be used for:

- The *triad:* to establish stability and direct energy in a masculine or feminine direction
- The *sign of infinity:* for balancing and connecting points
- The *nautilus or Fibonacci spiral:* for expansion or bringing into focus

The Triad

The triangle or triad is one of several significant shapes in the universe. It emits energy through its powerful frequency because it is based upon the Golden Mean, a vibrational pattern that serves as an interdimensional doorway through which energy emerges into matter on our plane of existence.

The triangle, equated with the number three, symbolizes the trinity of life: body, mind, and spirit as one unit—in other words, the elements of physical form, thought, and spirit. It also represents balance. If you think of the objects and physical positions that are reflections of the triangle (for example, the pyramid, lotus position, tree pose, Tree of Life, three-footed stool, holy trinity), you will find that each form reflects a strong structure of support and balance, which you can put to use in sound healing sessions.

In the Hindu tradition, a triangle pointing up symbolizes the male energy of fire, implementation, action, and manifestation. The downward-pointing triangle represents the female element of water, creativity, and receptivity. Superimposed on one another, they signify the unification of these two divine forces—the energy and principal of Creation.

Now let's use the triad to show you how to make use of a sacred shape in practice. (We'll come back to the triad in the discussion of layouts later in this chapter as well, getting into the types of bowls that are appropriate to use.)

A triad, of course, consists of three points, and you can view that linearly—as a two-dimensional triangle with two base points and an apex. For our purposes, the apex points either up toward the head or down toward the feet. But if you turn the triangle into a pyramid, you have created a three-dimensional envelope of sound, within which your intention works. The direction of the flow of energy depends on your orientation.

With that said, when you're working with a bowl, for example, there's a basic principle you can follow to intentionally direct energy using a triad. One is to strike the bowl away from the client (striking the apex toward the feet, as shown in the diagram, symbolically drawing energy from the person and into the earth, as a grounding method (feminine energy). Striking in the opposite direction, toward the head, moves energy up into the body (masculine energy). In general, you strike the plane first, establishing the base of the triad, and then you strike the apex—which will be above or below the base depending on the direction you are moving the energy. An exception is the head triad, where the apex at the crown is struck first, then the bowls that form the plane or base.

Possible Triads

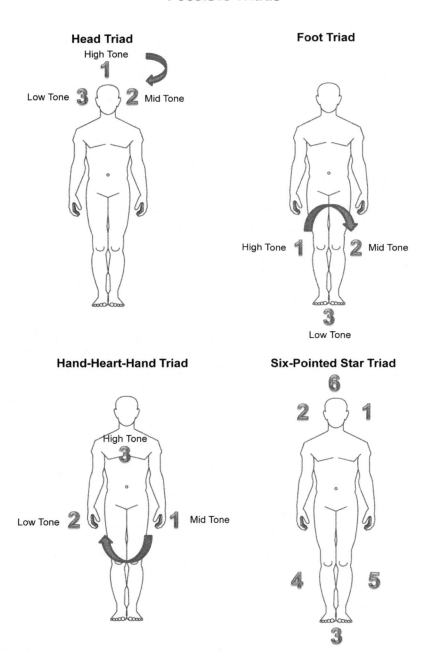

Head Triad

High Tone

1

Low Tone 3   2 Mid Tone

Foot Triad

High Tone 1   2 Mid Tone

3

Low Tone

Hand-Heart-Hand Triad

High Tone

3

Low Tone 2   1 Mid Tone

Six-Pointed Star Triad

6

2   1

4   5

3

When I start a session, I begin working with the head triad and an intention moving from divinity (the crown point). This first point at the crown can be seen as the still point from which the energy will move. Then I move from ear to ear in a clockwise direction; this represents the plane. The movement between these three points forms the head triad or triangle. Then, adding to this two-dimensional triad by holding a bowl above the head creates a three-dimensional form, symbolizing manifestation into the physical universe.

There are so many elements that come into play with the simple—but powerful—triangle. We will continue to touch on this as we move through the book.

The Infinity Shape, or Figure Eight

The infinity symbol usually starts at the center point and begins by moving either clockwise or counterclockwise, and then in the opposite direction as you pass over the center point. For example, if you are striking a ganta, you can start by striking it above the heart and then make your way around the head in a clockwise direction, crossing back over the heart and then moving counterclockwise to form the bottom half of the symbol. This movement will expand and balance energy. Start moving the ganta counterclockwise if the idea is to balance energy by drawing it inward. This symbol is an effective way to connecting any two points.

A simple technique for creating balance is to move the bowl in a figure-eight pattern over your client. I like to use a larger bowl for this, but you have to be really careful not to drop it, as this technique can throw you off balance, especially if you're using a heavier bowl.

During the course of this session you may find an area of very blocked energy. In this case you can play the ganta energetically over and around it.

The Nautilus (Spiral)

Similarly, the nautilus can be used to expand energy or draw it in. Starting in the center and spiraling outward expands energy. Starting on the outside and spiraling inward draws it in.

Common Layouts

Now we will look at a variety of introductory-level bowl layouts that are useful for vibrational healing. I use a total of sixteen bowls. You can do a great deal of good with only one, but it is best to have at least three to practice with—that's because three bowls allow you to create a triad, and it is in triads that many of the healing patterns are played.

That said, here I will assume a set of nine bowls, including:

- Three medium Manipuri or large Jambati bowls for the head (I recommend a medium-range Jambati bowl sound)
- One large grounding Jambati bowl for the feet (the lowest sound)
- Three medium/smaller bowls including a high-pitched Manipuri for the heart, and Thadobadis for the solar plexus, and sacrum, pitched high to low tones
- Two medium Manipuri bowls for the hands.

You can use a multitude of sacred geometry patterns when conducting a vibrational healing session. The one you choose depends on the client's need, your level of skill as a practitioner, and your understanding of sacred geometry. (For an advanced-level Kindle book on sacred geometry, visit the Store page on my website, tibetanbowlschool.com.) Here I'm covering the most basic of the bowl layouts and playing patterns. As you become more skilled, you will discover some of your own. And if you enroll in my certification program, you will learn many others.

The type of bowls you use will also depend on your client's needs. If they have physical pain or chronic illness, you may decide to use more Thadobadi bowls. If the client wishes to deepen their spiritual practice, gain clarity, or improve communication and relationships, Tibetan bowls may be a better choice. For the purpose of this book, I use a general mix of bowls.

Deeper into the Triad

First, choose three Jambati or Manipuri bowls that sound good together for your set around the head, pitched from highest to lowest. The preferred bowls for the head layout are mid-toned Jambati bowls, as they are neither too high nor too low pitched. You will place the highest at crown, then lower at left ear, and lowest at right ear. This is the pattern you play for the head bowls.

With the client on his or her back, place a bowl next to each ear and one at the crown. The bowls should be as close to the ears as possible but not touching any part of the body. This is the first and perhaps most important triad because this forms an "anchor" for the client.

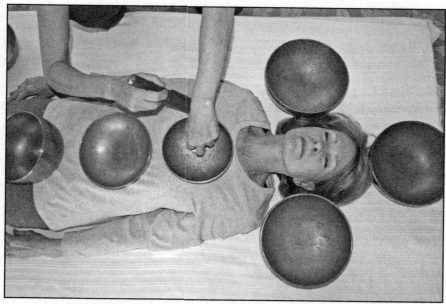

Triad around head, chakra bowls on heart, solar plexus, and abdomen.

An anchor is simply a pattern of sounds that is played repeatedly and becomes part of the client's cellular memory. We learn through repetition, so later when they hear that sound, they will remember the relaxing state they were in and be able to quickly access it.

It is vital to remember that when you strike the bowls, they will sound *many* times louder to the client than they do to you. Their ring will last a long time; you may not hear it, but your client will. So always strike the bowls around the head very softly, especially at first. You want to build up both the intensity and the pace very slowly.

Note: However slowly you start playing the bowls, slow down even more. Let them sing and vibrate for a long time before striking them again. This is soothing and pleasant for the client. *The biggest mistake new practitioners make is to strike the bowls too often and too hard. Focus on* listening *to the sound of the bowls and following their vibrations, versus* doing *techniques.*

As you listen, you may hear the bowls go into and out of harmony with one another, or a bowl may sound flat or out of tune. These are indications that it is best to work in that region of the body with those bowls until they remain harmonious with one another. Your bowls will sound differently with each client, so listening to them is vital. The pace and volume of your playing will gradually increase as you follow the shifts and direction of the energy.

You can continue playing the head triad for three to five minutes as you bring your client into a deep relaxation and trance state. Then you can create other triads on and around the body with other bowls, or move the head bowls to create them. Remember: if you move bowls, wait until they have *completely stopped* ringing (put your head close to them so you can hear this), and move them back to their original position from time to time to repeat the foundational anchor.

The second part of this basic triad has one bowl placed in each hand and one on the heart chakra. Watch out for fingers wrapping around or even touching the side of the hand bowls, as this will dull the vibration. If you notice this is happening, move the bowl farther out onto the fingers. Manipuri bowls ("heart bowls") are specified for this purpose, but if there is a big energetic block at the heart, you may wish to place a Bhutanese (Thadobadi) bowl there for some or all of the session. When you place a bowl directly on the body, it is preferable to put your index or third finger in the bowl to stabilize it when you strike it. There are different thoughts about what the fingers represent, but I consider the index finger to be the *air finger,* and the third finger to be the *fire finger.* It is important to be cognizant of which finger you are utilizing when working with the bowls in this manner. Using both together is a neutral hold.

You can now alternate between the two triads and create other triads from this basic pattern.

Basic layout.

The third part of the basic triad is at the feet. I place a very large bowl below but within a few inches of the feet and one on each side to create a triad. The amount of time I spend at the foot triad depends on how much the client needs grounding—whether they are in a highly emotional state, very anxious or worried, or "in their head" a lot. It's a good idea to return to the grounding bowl many times during your session. Remember to play the bowls with higher tones first and then move in sequence to the lower tones.

I also place bowls on the solar plexus and the sacrum (below the navel). If there is room I place a bowl on the root chakra too. Often, because there isn't enough room on most people's bodies for both, I use the sacral bowl and move it down to the root. At the root chakra, I usually place a towel on the thighs as close to the pubic bone or genitals as possible and put the bowl on that. Sometimes it is necessary to place something, such as a small piece of material, on one or both sides of this bowl to prevent it from tilting. Then I place a very small, high-pitched "third eye bowl" directly above the third eye (between the eyebrows) by holding it in my hand as close to that chakra as possible rather than placing it *on* the third eye.

Throat Bowl.

Some people have enough room at their throat that I can use a small bowl to clear and strengthen that energetic center. If not, I can hold the bowl directly above the throat to play it.

At this point I spend time playing triads around the body while clearing the chakras.

Working with Direction

Remember that *as you are playing, the direction you strike the bowls and your intention help direct the energy.*

Let me explain what I mean: If you want to move energy out of a body, you intend to direct it out and play accordingly. That is, you play from high to low tones, playing the apex of any triad (triangle) last and in the direction of the feet. If you want to create stability and grounding, you strike the bowls in the direction that awakens dormant energy and brings energy into the body. To do this, you play the two bowls at the base of the triad first and then the apex bowl last, going toward the head.

After you have established a series of patterns and intensities with the bowls by striking them, it is a good idea to circumnavigate the body by singing a bowl while walking around the client several times. You can also sing the bowl on specific areas to bring more harmony to those areas.

Singing bowl while creating figure-eight (infinity) pattern.

The sounds of the bowls combined with your skilled intuition, the signals you get from watching your client, and the conversation you had prior to the session help you determine where and when you do what. And if you have conducted a tingshas diagnosis, this will certainly serve as a guide. Then you can utilize the patterns of sacred geometry to create the energy shifts that will move your practice partners and clients toward harmony and wholeness.

Part III

Sound Healing and the Chakras

In this part of the book, you will learn how to integrate working with the major energy centers of the body into your sound healing practice. These centers are called chakras (a name derived from the Sanskrit word for "wheel"), and there are seven primary ones located from the base of the spine to the crown of the head. There are actually several other, more minor chakras, but the main seven are plenty for beginners to explore and we will restrict our discussion to these. If after working with these chakras for some time, you would like to explore other chakra systems, I encourage you to do so and consider incorporating them into your practice as well. Cyndi Dale has written at length about the additional energy centers in the body, and I highly recommend her books on the subject. But you can also do an Internet search on "twelve chakra system" and "114 chakras and find a wealth of information.

Chakra Work in a Sound Healing Session: General Principles

There are many ways to work with each chakra using the foundational principles of sound healing and employing each sacred sound tool appropriately. You will find specific suggestions for working with the tingshas, ganta and dorje, and bowls in each chakra chapter. In general, however, I invite you to follow these guidelines.

Make sure that your focus is not myopic—in other words, don't restrict yourself in a session to balancing a particular chakra. Even if the tingshas and your intuition tell you that you need to pay attention to one or another of them, be sure that you're also taking in the whole person. Remember: You are always holding the space for your clients to be in their wholeness. They are much greater than any one chakra.

As is true with all clients and the healing they need, when you are assessing whether a chakra needs work it is important to pay attention to body language and breathing. And listen not only to what the client says but how they say it—tone and rhythm of voice. This kind of attention will help you see or sense whether a chakra is blocked, clear, or overactive before you even touch the instruments. There are many ways to recognize the nuances of a chakra. The sacred sound instruments will certainly indicate imbalance, but it is good to observe all aspects of a person to get the most complete picture possible, as many interrelationships are at play here.

When you are assessing imbalances in the chakras, it is important not to be too literal—symbolism and subtlety are important too—or to expect certain typical ailments to be involved. A blocked sacral chakra could manifest as a sexual disorder (a condition that is explicitly associated with the sacral chakra), for instance, but it may not. It might manifest as illness in the throat, for example, when someone has swallowed so many external ideas about themselves, other people's expectations, and other people's truths that she has none left for herself; the illness of the throat then becomes a pathway back to her own truth. Become familiar with the characteristics of each chakra to see how one might affect another.

The point here is that when we work with chakras, even though each has its own set of attributes, we don't really work with just one chakra at a time. Apply the fundamental Buddhist principle that underlies sound healing: the interrelationship of all things.

As a practical matter, when you are working with a very sensitive area like the root chakra, understand that you can approach it indirectly by using reflex points that refer to that area. In taking this approach, you are making use of an energetic versus a physical connection, and physical contact with a sensitive area is not required. By reflex points, I am referring to working with the long element lines of the body (see the first chapter in this section on polarity) as a way to work energetically and remotely with a particular chakra.

For example, if you are working with the throat chakra and you want to add some earth energy there, since you don't want to place a bowl or ganta directly on the throat, you could work that chakra through the pinky finger or the little toe, both of which represent the earth element. The same approach would work with the root chakra, which you also do not want to physically touch. It reflexes to the feet, the neck, the pinky finger, and the little finger and toe.

As another practical matter, also remember that chakras are funnel shaped and open to both the front and back of the body, so you can do chakra work on either the front or back of the body, or both.

Don't forget crystals when you're choosing ways to work with the chakras. In the beginning of the session, you can clear the chakras from the crown on down with a crystal dorje, and then do your balancing, strengthening, and harmonizing work. Oftentimes when I'm starting with the occipital hold, I might put crystals on all the chakras, and then do the occipital hold for about forty-five seconds or a minute. You will need several crystals to do this. (I can help you select the best crystal dorje for your needs—see Further Resources.)

Finally, you will discover that while the sacred instruments are of course essential to sound healing work, other tools are important as well. Exploring your practice partner's mind/body state verbally, for example, helps you determine what instrument work to include in a session. That's why in each chapter you will find questions you might choose to ask your partner to help identify the kinds of shifts they may need to help them along on their path to healing and wholeness.

I think you will find that, after a little practice, working with these energy centers will become fundamental to your sound healing sessions—they certainly are in my own practice. It is for this reason that I have devoted several chapters to developing an understanding of them.

Chapter 8
THE POLARITIES OF THE BODY

Part of what I bring to sound healing work is my training in polarity therapy, and when it comes to working with chakras, the principles of this healing modality will serve you well. That's why we will start the section on chakras with a discussion of polarity.

Just as magnets have polarity—a positive pole and a negative pole—all electromagnetic fields of energy have polarity, including the human body. The positive pole is not good and the negative is not bad; the poles are simply positive or negative in relation to one another. Polarity therapy is a healing modality whose purpose is "realigning the body to be in harmony with the soul"[4] by working with the positive and negative points of the body's natural energy field.

Shifting the energy field of the body is energy medicine that, like sacred sound, works on every level: spiritual, physical, and emotional. Here, I will introduce you to some of the simpler aspects of the body's polarities so you can integrate these principles into your sessions. More techniques related to polarities are available in the Advanced 1 workshop (see the Resources section).

Note that when we work with subtle energy systems such as the auric field (the field of energy around the physical body) and the etheric body (the layer of the auric field closest to the physical body), we are working with electromagnetic fields. These means we do not *have* to touch the body (though we can). This is because when our intention is focused and strong the nervous system will respond.

I refer to the positive and negative energetic poles of the body as *elemental long lines* because each of the lines represents one of the five elements: ether, air, fire, water, and earth. Each of the elements corresponds to an organ system or other area of the body, and each element can be in a balanced, expanded, or contracted state. There can be too much or too little of each element present. There are different ways to work with these elements to create balance during a session. Some involve hand placement and some involve using the ganta.

I usually work with the elements before I place any bowls on the body. That is, I work with the ganta over the long lines and balance the elements through hand placement. But there are many other ways to work the polarity and the elements into a session.

Elemental Long Lines

The long vertical lines of the body progress from the center of the body outward. Referring to the following diagram, you can see that the central line of the body, the ether line, begins at the crown and goes all the way down to the big toe. The first line of energy to either side of ether is air, ending at the second toe; the next one is fire, ending at the middle toe; and the next in succession is water, ending at the fourth toe. Finally we have the earth line, which runs along the outer edge of the body and ends at the little toe. To clear an element, you can use the ganta to move energy from top to bottom along its corresponding long line.

Each element also has a series of reflex points on the body: that is, points that represent the positive and negative energy fields of the five elements in the body. You can place your hands (or crystals) on these points to establish balance. In polarity therapy, these placements are called *tridoshas*.

Alternatively, you can work on these points in the auric and etheric fields just a few inches above the body.

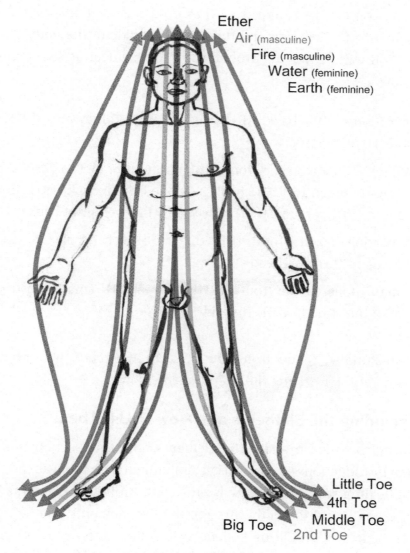

Ether
Air (masculine)
Fire (masculine)
Water (feminine)
Earth (feminine)

Little Toe
4th Toe
Middle Toe
Big Toe   2nd Toe

Elemental long lines.

Always work with the right hand (RH, projecting energy) at the bottom—closer to the feet—and the left hand (LH, receiving energy) at the top, closer to the head. Do not cross your hands to do this. If you position yourself on the right side of the client's body when they are lying on their back, you should be fine. Most tridoshas are done on the front of the body when the client is on their back. However, working with the air element is always done on the back, and water has protocols for both front and back of the body. Do the left side and then the right side of the body with each tridosha. You will be moving around the body connecting two points with your hands:

> **Air** (done on the back): (RH) ankle to (LH) kidney area, (RH) kidney to (LH) shoulder
>
> **Water** 1. (done on the front): (RH) bottom of foot to (LH) abdomen, (RH) abdomen to (LH) chest; 2. (done on the back) (RH) bottom of foot to (LH) sacrum, (RH) sacrum to (LH) center of back
>
> **Fire** (done on the front): (RH) thigh to (LH) solar plexus, (RH) solar plexus to (LH) forehead
>
> **Earth** (done on the front): (RH) knee to (LH) small intestine, (RH) small intestine to (LH) thyroid

This technique, taken from *The Polarity Workbook* by Nancy Anna Risley, is helpful for getting the client to slow down.

Understanding the Elements and How to Use Them

There is much to learn about the elements, and this section will be the briefest of introductions so you can get acquainted with them as they pertain to sound healing sessions. Energy is projected through the chakras into the physical domain and the body through the five elements of ether, air, fire, water, and earth. It would be beneficial to reflect upon your observations of the character of each element. Imagine that element in a balanced state, then overactive, and then underactive.

Water, for example, can be flowing smoothly through a stream, gushing in destructive torrents, or in scarce supply during a drought. This reflection will inform how you work with the element in your session. Use what you know about direction and patterns of sacred geometry (see Chapter 00) to balance, strengthen, or dispel/release the energy of any element. You can use a tridosha to balance any element, and then follow with the ganta and dorje and bowls, taking into account not only layouts and direction, but *how* you play each instrument: using a strong earthy touch, a light touch, or something else. For example, singing a bowl is soothing, and I associate it with water energy. If I wanted to move energy in a watery manner, I would probably sing rather than strike a bowl or ganta.

Ether

Ether represents free flow, expansiveness, and freedom of expression in all its forms. The ether pathway is located down the central channel of the body. Ether is an idea, an element, and a way of touching someone. Working with ether is effective when someone feels like they're trapped or life has dumped on them. Blocked ether might be seen as an inability to move forward, anxiety, feeling boxed in, or claustrophobia. Clearing and expanding ether can help give your practice partner a sense of perspective—a sense of timelessness and spaciousness—when they feel like they're in a black hole.

Ether energy is reflexed in all the joints of the body. To work with this element, first clear the ether long line (striking a ganta from the crown down the central channel several times). Then work on whatever chakra or energy center needs strengthening or balancing. When that work is complete, you can move the energy outward into the ethers, thus expanding the work you have done and bringing it into a larger context. I think of ether as something to expand into, so using a clockwise spiral with a ganta is effective for doing that.

Air

The quality of the air element is volatility; air moves and changes all the time. It is associated with the nervous system, whose element is mainly air. Air also represents the lungs, heart, and kidneys (which balance the pH of the blood), as well as the shoulders and ankles.

Unbalanced air could manifest as confused thinking, mental anxiety, lack of commitment or clarity, poor follow-through, volatility of character (dishonesty, lack of integrity), or indecisiveness. Think of someone who is always changing jobs because they just can't give themselves to anything and stay with it, or someone who complains a lot. Air that is out of balance is like a mental traffic jam.

What brings the air element into balance will vary according to the person. Some people need fire to energize the air element—this would be the case if they demonstrate stagnant thinking or depression. Some might need earth energy for grounding and maybe some water to create a flow versus scattered thinking.

Fire

Fire affects the motor and sympathetic nervous systems and is associated with the head, solar plexus (stomach and digestion), and thighs. The fire pathway stores our anger (associated with the liver) and is the conduit for our creativity. The head is the top end of the fire line, the stomach and digestive systems are the mid-range of that element, and the thighs are the bottom end.

Fire can manifest as pent-up energy, unfulfilled thoughts or emotions, or a self-defeating, not self-fulfilling, attitude. Some of the attributes of this element include a need for power, a short fuse, and low ideals. Anger is an essential element, an indicator that lets us know what is out of balance and needs to be cleansed in order to make room for something better. Anger is masculine in nature and destroys what does not support us so that new growth (creative energy) can take place.

The tridosha for fire can be effective to balance that element, but if fever, inflammation, infection, or high blood pressure is present, follow up with the ganta, dorje, and bowls while holding the intention of cooling and diminishing, making sure to work with the apex of the triads in the feminine or downward position. (See the illustrations on pages 107 to 108.)

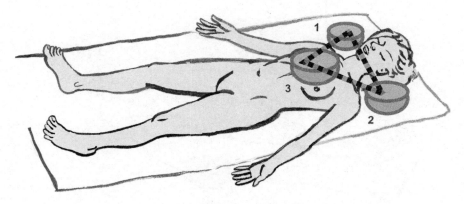

Descending: Heart triad.

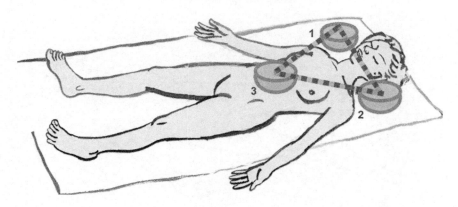

Descending: Solar plexis triad.

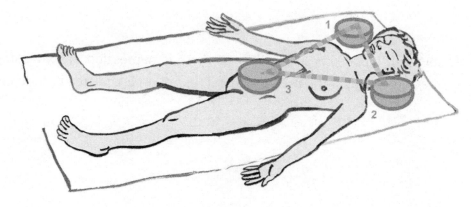

Descending: Sacral triad.

THE POLARITIES OF THE BODY **109**

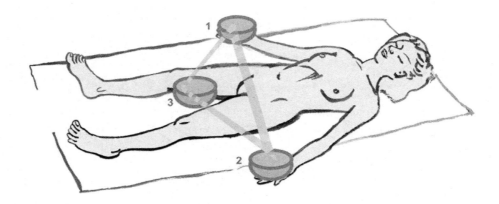

Descending: Root triad.

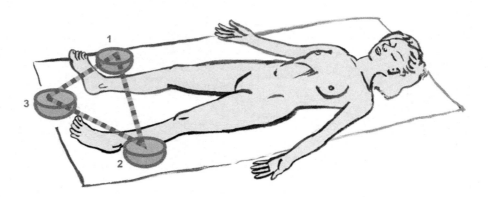

Descending: Grounding triad.

If, however, blood pressure is low or there is depression or exhaustion, then some energizing of the fire points and the solar plexus area is called for.

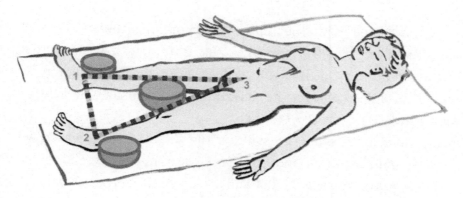

Ascending: Ankle-ankle-root triad.

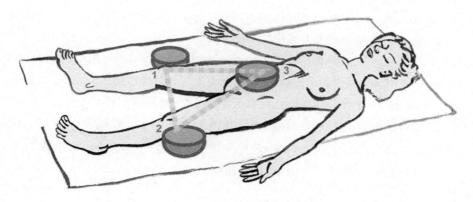

Ascending: Knee-knee-sacrum triad.

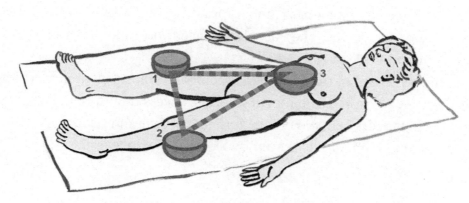

Ascending: Knee-knee-solar plexis triad.

Water

Water is associated with the reproductive organs (the sacral or second chakra), the heart chakra, and the feet. It is also associated with the parasympathetic nervous system, and areas of the body that reflect the timeline of our life. Whatever the case, the water tridosha will bring balance to that element.

Water blockage is often an issue for the sacral chakra, where we store our deepest sadness, grief, and trauma. Lack of nurturing and love causes us to store a fragile system of trust and sense of self-worth here. If a client is having a lot of trouble with their water pathway, working with the sacrum will help them with acceptance and integration of their feelings about their sexuality and will balance their male and female sides. If there's a cognitive association—a mental and cellular aspect coming together—a memory or emotion that has been stored in the sacrum may emerge to be released.

In more advanced work you can use visualizations to balance water. Water work is relaxing and restores a sense of flow. If water is dammed up, you can sometimes use another element such as air or earth to balance it out. But sometimes when water is blocked you might instead choose to work to restore that sense of the flowing water rather than addressing the blockage.

If someone is too watery, collapsing into tears every five minutes and having no control of their emotions, you want to create some strengthening. This client needs rootedness and grounding, as well as some fire to neutralize excess water. They absolutely need form too, so strengthening earth is important as well.

At the other end of the spectrum is someone whose emotions are stuck, who can't cry or express their feelings, lacks access to intuition, lacks trust, is unable to nurture self and others, has a lot of fear and poor relationships, goes from job to job, or has sexual issues or abundance issues.

Earth

Earth is associated with physical form and relates to the throat, the elimination system, and the knees. Affecting earth issues takes time because of this element's density and slow-moving nature (imagine moving through clay). Issues in the earth pathway may manifest as difficult relationships with first family (parents, children, and siblings—the family structure), constipation (holding on to resentment), bone issues (structure), weight issues, and depression. Some of the nonphysical aspects of unbalanced earth include stubbornness, being overly critical, being stuck in one's ways, and lacking playfulness and fun.

So how do you move a mountain? A little bit at a time, with lots of patience. Using the earth tridosha would be effective in helping the client relax and release what they have been holding on to for a long time. Clacking the ganta gently but persistently at the root and/or feet is a good way to start breaking up stuck earth energy.

I encourage you to keep the principles of polarity in mind as you explore working with the chakras in the following six chapters. Not only do these principles offer important context for thinking about the qualities, direction, and flow of energy in the body, but they also help remind you of the interconnection between all things—including the chakras' connection with one another—and to view the energy body as a whole even as you may be choose to emphasize a specific chakra.

Chapter 9
THE FIRST OR ROOT CHAKRA

Location and Qualities of the Root Chakra

The root chakra is located at the base of the spine—we sit on the root chakra. It is a complex energy center that can hold blockages originating in early childhood. It is rare to come across someone who does not have some issues in this area. Because of its nature, location, and what it controls, as a sound healing practitioner you must take care to create a safe environment when working with the root chakra.

If you have a bowl collection that is based on notes, it's handy to know that the root chakra resonates to the note of C, though in my practice I pay more attention to tone and harmonics than notes. The root chakra is identified with the color red, the element of the earth, the physical process of elimination, the bladder, and the rectum. It is associated with your relationship to survival and feelings of safety in the world.

The root chakra is about the survival of the species, issues of community, home, food, and basic physical needs. It is the center of material life. On a symbolic level, it represents the inner infant who simply needs and is at the mercy of caretakers and the larger world around her. Here you can find the cellular memory of deep-rooted, survival-related fear. So, if you think in terms of how you would work with an infant, it becomes clear that it's not something you can do with a heavy hand.

Remember that earth is the densest element to work with. It sometimes feels like clay and is extremely slow moving. It can get very clogged up. What this means for you is that this area will often require a series of sessions before there is a shift. Even so, although it is unlikely you will clear a root chakra issue in a single session, including grounding as part of every session is a good idea.

The root chakra is always connected to the earth, but there is a lot of interference here and this area often requires a substantial amount of clearing. One way to work with the root chakra is as close to the groin as possible with bowls between the legs in a spread-eagle fashion. It's a very vulnerable position and you need to have established a lot of trust with your client or practice partner. This is not a layout to do in the first couple of sessions. For the first sessions you can simply place a bowl on top of the thighs near the root to work.

What a Blocked or Overactive Root Chakra Looks Like

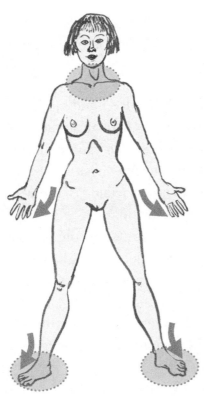

Root chakra reflex points.

The root chakra is where a great deal of our fear and our sense of deficiency and powerlessness are stored. I have noticed that many women have a sense of dependency, a feeling that their survival is somehow linked up with needing someone else to take care of them. This can also manifest as the need to be defined by others and reflect other people's images of us back upon ourselves.

These are signs of root chakra blockage, which can manifest as having little or no ego, identity, or sense of self-worth. The origin of this may be that the person's parents or community didn't support their having a strong sense of self. People whose root chakra is blocked are often looking for approval, attention, and validation. In the Tibetan Buddhist tradition, this is reflected in an entity called the "hungry ghost": a small, funny-looking person with a huge belly and a tiny mouth who always needs to eat. No matter how much he eats, his hunger is never satisfied. Symbolically, the hungry ghost can be seen as living in the root chakra. When the root chakra is blocked, it is not unusual for people to give away their power to perceived fears that then block creativity. They hold the view that the world is not a safe place.

The first and second chakras are closely related, but there are differences. First chakra issues are really fundamental. Think of the first chakra as related to physical needs, shelter, and about our sense of being safe—or unsafe—in the world. If instead a person feels "I am a victim of this horrible world and everything is always against me," that's the first chakra speaking.

An overactive root chakra, by contrast, can cause hyperactivity, recklessness, sexual obsessiveness, or fixations such as smoking. Oftentimes, hyperactivity—the need to do, do, do all the time—is a smokescreen for lack of self-worth. The obsessive need to create is also a way to validate oneself all the time.

In your conversations and observations during sessions, be aware of how much your client:

- Is focused on and repeats negative belief systems or patterns
- Judges other people (often to build themselves up)
- Feels ungrounded by other people's opinions
- Lives from other people's expectations without having a say in it themselves
- Feels powerless

These are all indicators of a root chakra issue.

What an Open and Clear Root Chakra Looks Like

One indication of a clear root chakra is how connected someone feels to others and the world around them. Clients often express wanting connection and explicitly say, "I don't feel connected." Someone with an open and clear root chakra has a feeling of belonging, of connectedness to the universe. They feel able to hold their power and have a sense of having enough; the cup is always half full. They come from a stance of security, not of lack. They're able to walk on their own two feet without constant reassurance from others.

Questions for Exploring Root Chakra Issues

Questions you might ask clients to help bring more consciousness to situations are:

- Do you feel safe? In what situations?
- How can you validate yourself?
- What do you need to feel safe?

- How would it feel to be perfectly nourished with your basic needs fulfilled?

If the answer indicates a feeling of safety and belonging in the world, that's great. By comparison, if the answer indicates the person needs a lot of stuff, money, validation, or power to feel connected and safe, then you've got some root chakra issues.

Are they really living or just in survival mode? Do they have constant issues with money and relationships and security? Always look for this kind of path, because answers to these questions can lead to powerful intentions to hold in working with the root chakra.

The Root Chakra: Doing the Work

As I mentioned earlier, be very careful when you work with the root chakra. People often tense up the muscles around their sexual center. It can be helpful to use breath to assist them in relaxing and releasing. You can invite them to exhale all the way from their crown down through the bottoms of their feet—like a tree growing roots— and repeat the anchoring pattern and the foot triad several times while they do this.

Rooting through breath.

Here are a few of the many possible options when working with the root chakra. Remember that the root is constantly in connection with the earth, but the connection gets interrupted all the time. You need to clear, ground, and expand a sense of trust. After clearing and grounding, you might create clockwise spirals starting at the root to expand a sense of trust into the world. You can clack the ganta softly in rhythmic patterns to break up some of the very stuck and heavy energy here and then strike it while creating clockwise spirals to further release stuck energy. You might do a figure-eight

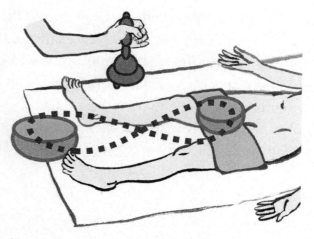

Root figure 8 with ganta.

pattern (the infinity symbol) between the feet and the root chakra to establish a stronger, flowing connection to the earth.

Remember that it's the clearing and foundational work and then the re-anchoring in the triads around the head that reestablish a strong base, something those with root chakra issues lack. For this reason, I recommend you keep going back to the head triad to help "set" the work you are doing in the person's consciousness and cellular memory.

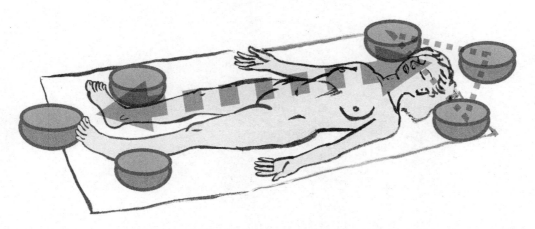

Return to head triad.

With that said, between the groin and the earth, there can be a lot going on that you want to ground. For example, the knees contain the memory of first family (the blood family we were born into: mother, father, sister, brother) and it's probably a safe bet to imagine that root chakra issues originated there. So that's a good starting point. You might create a pattern of hip, hip, root, with the apex of that triad being the root. The hips are about strong movement forward.

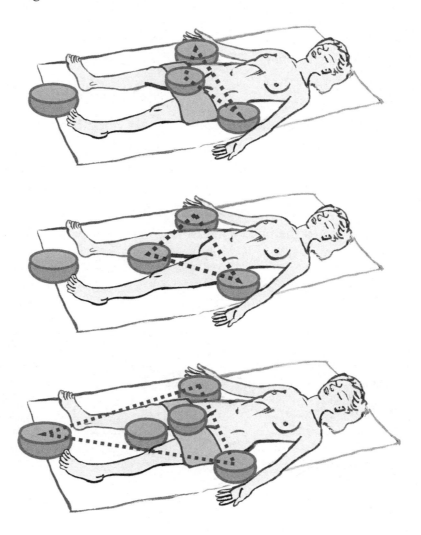

Hip-hip-root, hip-hip-knee, hip-hip-foot triads.

Then you can work your way down: hip, hip, knee (with a bowl between the knees) and then hip, hip, foot bowl.

Remember also that the neck is a reflex point to the root and is about self-expression, sound, self-judgment, or truth, reconnecting with one's own self-expression rather than the expression of community. You want to release nonproductive elements through the root chakra and replace the inner voice of constant putdowns with the voice of encouragement.

For clients with reproductive problems, you can use the ganta and dorje to help move the energy in that area. Placing the dorje horizontally between the hips on the sacrum is a means of helping to balance the ovaries. Remember that where there is a root issue, it probably affects the sacrum.

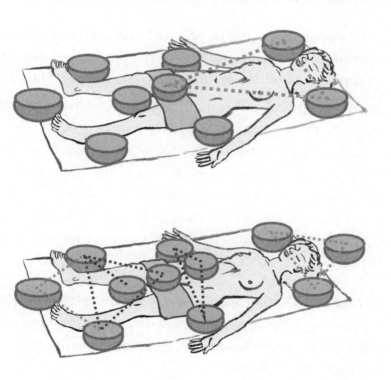

Neck-neck-root and upward triads.

Then you can work your way back up, starting with the foot bowl and creating triads with the apex on top to move the energy back up the body. I would include working with the sacrum as part of the work with the root chakra: clearing it, singing it for a long time, or sending the energy out or up through intention.

It is soothing to sing a bowl for a long time on the root and sacrum; people will often relax into that, thereby releasing the muscles in that area. Many people hold tension in the muscles around their sexual organs without even being aware of it. If you put a blanket on the client, you can usually place a bowl on the legs just below the root and it will not fall through.

Student Questions

I will close this chapter with a few questions I have received from students that pertain to root chakra work.

In yoga, we're about standing on the feet and really feeling the ground, and I know that earth energy and the root chakra are related. Do you ever work with someone standing up or is it strictly a lying-down thing?

When you are grounded and comfortable with the basic principles, they can be integrated into other modalities in so many ways. I have often played for yoga classes, and it is very powerful to marry the bowl patterns and rhythms to the yoga poses, or to walk around the room and hold a bowl near a person who is in a pose to strengthen or move more energy within that pose. As you progress in this work you will be working with people sitting, lying on their sides, or even in beds so certainly you will adapt the work to the situation at hand.

If you're working with somebody who has pronounced root chakra issues, would you tend to focus most of the session on that and spend minimal time balancing the other chakras, or do you tend to try to keep the balance in your allotment of time?

The issues associated with the root chakra can manifest in a lot of ways that impact other chakras. A lot depends on the client and the feedback you are getting from the instruments on the body. The root chakra covers a lot of personal space. So if you're doing a lot of work on the root chakra, especially if you're working directly on it rather than holding the bowl above it, and if the client is not trusting, you can create even more fear than was present in that area before.

For example, if someone has been raped and that chakra is very stuck, placing a large bowl in between their legs and on their sacrum may be too powerful. In that situation it would be better to work with the feet, doing a lot of grounding and establishing a sense of safety and comfort, and then perhaps working on reflex areas. Look at other less vulnerable chakras to start the release with—maybe the heart or the throat—and then as the energies start flowing more naturally, you can move to include the root chakra. Your first step in these types of cases is to help the client relax and release so that when you start doing the root chakra work, they feel more welcoming of the work and less defensive. The root chakra may be the last place you get to and it will be the last place to clear after several sessions.

Only when it seems safe would I try to spend more time there than in other places. Remember this: the *sound* of the bowls will give you most of the information you need to work with, so listen carefully to the instruments as you work.

You can also use other modalities if you include them in your practice: massage, touch, laying on of hands, your voice as a soothing instrument. All of these things are really helpful with clients who have a lot of trust issues.

Do higher-pitch bowls ever resonate well with lower chakras, or does the use of them just enhance upper chakra overactivity?

The body is surrounded by layers of energy. Normally, the root chakra would call for the lower-tone bowls. But at times you might sense that perhaps someone is just about to break through their issue, and a higher tone might be just the thing to bring them to that next level. This might happen after you've cleared the root chakra and you want to resonate something that's higher. Your intention is to marry that root chakra to a higher level of itself, and then to a more spiritual level where there is a clear passage between crown and root. In cases like this, higher-pitched bowls are perfectly acceptable.

Chapter 10
THE SECOND OR SACRAL CHAKRA

Location and Qualities of the Sacral Chakra

The second or sacral chakra is located a bit below the navel where the second from the bottom dot is on the diagram. It is associated with the color orange. The sacral chakra corresponds to the element of water, the Divine Feminine, unconditional love, wisdom, and cycles of creativity. It also encompasses our sexual center, the functions of the reproductive glands, and the pelvic area in general and is the energetic center of one-on-one relationships.

This chakra is the home of trust—and money issues; there is a joke that our bank account is really in our lower back. It is the foundational area of the energetic flow. Our emotional drive is stored here and holds the memory of how well or how poorly we were nurtured as children, along with how well we nurture ourselves and others. It is the warehouse for grief, stuck emotions, trauma, and more. Symbolically, the sacrum represents the inner toddler to about five years old, so familial issues and messages, especially the unconscious messages we received when we were in our most formative years, are stored here.

What a Blocked or Overactive Sacral Chakra Looks Like

Blocked sacral chakra issues include fear and stress around prosperity, abundance, and security. This could manifest as lower back pain, antisocial tendencies, or being isolated from others. Life doesn't seem to flow. Blocked chakras can also show up as repeated interpersonal conflicts. A blocked sacral chakra could be reflected by trouble with trusting or opening up to other people. It can also manifest as a challenge in maintaining intimate, long-lasting relationships with loved ones. In addition, it can show up as difficulties conceiving, or blocked creativity.

Oftentimes we hurt ourselves because we keep things bottled up inside, sometimes for a lifetime. When something feels hurtful or a heart is broken because of betrayal, it is often stuffed inside rather than expressing that hurt. Other chakras might be impacted by this as well, but keeping things inside can often create a blockage in the second chakra.

For a woman in particular, the second chakra and the throat are very connected, and a blocked sacral chakra can manifest as difficulties expressing herself, complaining of pain in her throat, or feeling like she is choking, or not standing up for her truth. There is a lot being "swallowed" and that discomfort, resentment, grief, or pain lives in the sacrum instead of being expressed via the throat.

An overactive second chakra can cause a lot of fluttering during the tingshas diagnosis. It can present as a need to control others, and that can be through positive or negative acts (for example, some people control others through a lot of gift giving, a form of manipulation). Other examples might be people who are power or money hungry. They could also be overly lustful, sexually controlling, or arrogant. These would also reflect in the solar plexus, the area of will.

In your conversations and observations during sessions be aware of how much your client:

- Was nurtured as a child
- Is able to nurture others (and how they nurture)
- Can be controlled, or controls others, through money
- Has codependent relationships with people or substances
- Enjoys a healthy sexual life
- Feels a sense of trust in relationship to people and the world
- Exhibits controlling behavior

For example, a lot of cancer patients have sacral issues because they are givers. They get their power through giving, giving, giving, baking too many brownies, always saying yes as a way of defining themselves and making sure they are included. But this way of giving comes at a cost. That is, they give out of obligation and expectation and do not attend to themselves the way they attend to others. They need to establish boundaries and learn how to receive. Often they need to learn to let go of control and allow things to be as they are.

For example, a woman who has cancer in her sacrum might meditate for five hours a day, working so hard to be in control of her situation that she overdoes it. She needs help in learning how to allow things to unfold and be a witness to her process. Then she can make decisions based on what would be best for her well-being without feeling like she always needs to control the outcome. This doesn't mean doing nothing, but she will learn to do what is best for herself in the moment rather than taking action as a means to control an outcome.

What an Open and Clear Sacral Chakra Looks Like

Some of the key elements of a clear second chakra include happiness in relationships, being open, and not having trust issues with significant people in one's life. Other clues are the ability to be intimate with others, happiness with work and money, a sense of abundance and prosperity, and the ability to provide for oneself, maintain a sense of security, and generally see the cup as half full. Having a clear second chakra can also be a matter of being able to express oneself in a social and open way.

Questions for Exploring Sacral Chakra Issues

- Where do you feel supported and unsupported in life?
- What aspects of your life are controlled by other people's expectations?
- What recurring patterns do you notice in your relationships?
- Are you content with the level of intimacy you have it your relationships?

Are Addictions a Second Chakra Issue?

Sexual and gambling addictions are definitely clear indicators of an overactive sacral chakra. Basically, when people have an addiction, their essence or authentic self is at odds with their behaviors and the personality they manifest. There is often an unconscious belief in unworthiness, and they may choose to do things that reinforce that belief. This can come from issues in childhood: from any situation where they felt they needed to escape—to be someone or somewhere else. Shopaholics have the same issues, as does anybody who feels compelled to do something that will ultimately make them feel bad about themselves, thereby supporting their unconscious belief that they are unworthy and damaged.

The Sacral Chakra: Doing the Work

Now we know a bit more about how the second chakra presents and how issues with the second chakra (blocked or overactive) can be identified. Let's look at some ways we can help people expand, release, connect, and align themselves toward a position of wellness.

Working on the sacrum with the ganta is effective for a couple of reasons: The sacrum represents the feminine and the element of water, and the ganta also symbolizes the aspects of the Divine Feminine. The task of the ganta and the dorje is to *move* energy. And who doesn't have some stuck energy to move due to negative thought patterns, behaviors, or belief systems about themselves? Almost everyone does.

Figure 8 pattern and clockwise ganta spiral.

Remember that intention is a vital part of how you do what you do in a sound healing session. And note that the sacrum is a center point of the patterns of sacred geometry that you can use. You can place the dorje between the heart and the sacrum in a vertical position to bring heart energy to the sacrum. You can make the sign of infinity (the figure-eight pattern) by gently striking the ganta and moving it vertically, connecting the heart chakra to the sacrum through the solar plexus.

You can make ganta spirals clockwise with the idea of releasing fearful energy, creating a sense of expansiveness and space in that chakra for good healing energy. This will make room for positive, healing energy to be accessed.

After moving the energy around the sacral chakra with the ganta, you can support that work with the bowls by creating triads going toward the grounding bowl (foot bowl). Why? Because this will bring the healing, spiritual energy from the crown down through the chakras into the sacrum and out, creating that nice chakra flush from top to bottom. (Remember that in a triad, the base of the triangle is played first and the apex last—an exception is the head triad.) It is effective to play patterns in series of three (three, six, nine, or other multiples of three).

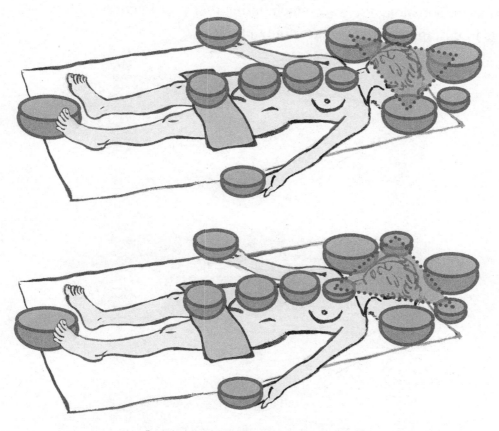

Crown triad and head-head-heart.

You can also use five bowls around the head. Place one bowl above each of the bowls so it forms an arch, with the highest tone right above the crown and the lowest tone being the last bowl played. This means that the tones would go from higher to lower.

Start with the crown chakra, then head-head-heart, and then ear-ear-heart. Then perhaps crown-heart-solar, then hand-hand-sacrum, then ear-ear-root, ear-ear-foot.

Then work down the chakras from crown to foot. You can place the dorje in a vertical position between the heart and sacrum or right next to the body. As when you work with all the chakras, there are so many possibilities and each technique you choose depends on the situation at hand. These are just some options to try while listening to the bowls for information along the way, remembering that your intention as you work is as important as what you are doing physically.

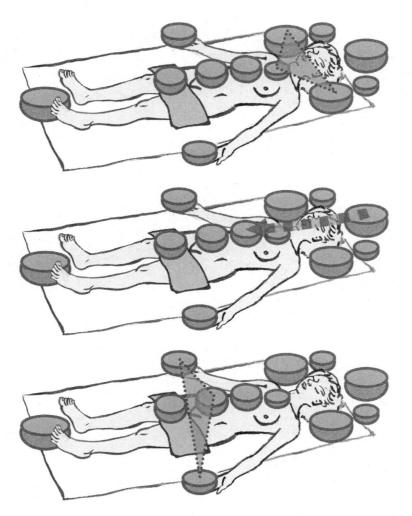

Ear-ear-heart, crown-heart-solar plexus, and hand-hand-sacrum.

You might then try head-throat-sacrum-foot, and when those are aligned, then head-throat-heart-sacrum. Hold the throat bowl above and close to the throat rather than trying to place it directly on the throat. The throat and sacrum have such an important connection that you can also put a bowl on either side of the throat and do throat-throat-sacrum. Placing a tiny crystal on the throat will amplify the bowl or ganta work. Then do a series to include throat-sacrum, throat-heart-sacrum, throat-heart-solar-sacrum.

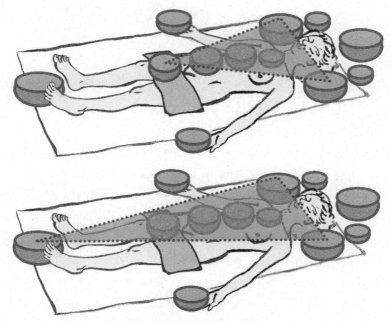

Ear-ear-root, and ear-ear-foot.

It is best to use a lower-toned Thadobadi (Bhutanese) bowl on the sacrum because it offers a direct vibration into the sacrum and is most effective for physical healing. There are situations where singing a Jambati grounding bowl is helpful as well. In that case, it is necessary to remove both the sacral and solar plexus bowls to make room for the larger Jambati. The reason for doing that is to bring a higher consciousness to the sacrum rather than work on the more physical aspects best addressed with a Thadobadi bowl.

If you have a lot of bowls, you can place them outside the hips to do a hip-hip-foot as well.

Take your time when you get a nice harmonic flow going. Remember to really listen to the instruments, and if a bowl sounds dull, discordant, or sharp, keep working to bring it into the harmonic fold.

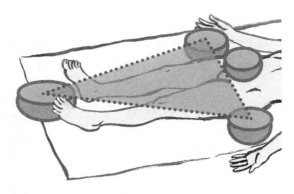

Hip-hip-foot.

If you want to bring energy up, create triads with the two bowls on either side of the feet as a base and work your way up. You can move bowls around if you don't have a lot of them. Maybe put one outside each knee so you can play knee-knee-sacrum. The knees in general represent first family issues, so that's a strong connection between the sacrum and the knees.

These are just several examples of what can be done with the sacral chakra by working with the basic principles. If the sacrum is clear and there is already sense of spaciousness there, you might envision orange light nourishing and strengthening the sacrum. That's when it would be good to work with bringing the energy back up, or even expanding it outward with spirals.

Chapter 11
THE THIRD OR SOLAR PLEXUS CHAKRA

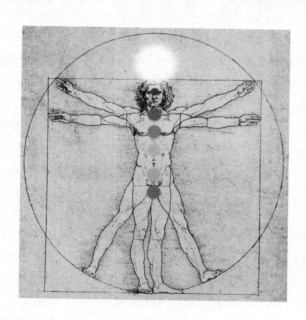

Location and Qualities of the Solar Plexus Chakra

The third chakra is located at the solar plexus, indicated by the third dot from the bottom on the chart. It resonates with the color yellow. In some traditions this chakra resonates to the tone of E. The solar plexus chakra represents the element of fire and masculine energy, and it impacts the bowels, digestive system, and stomach—systems that are responsible for our whole body's well-being. It reigns over the adrenal glands, which control vitality and how well the motor nervous system runs, the energy to get up and go, and the liver, which cleans up old blood cells and regulates the digestive process. Symbolically, it reflects the inner adolescent, the center of will, and the place where we store our sacred contracts: the seat of our self-esteem and how we honor ourselves.

The Importance of Honoring Yourself

Because the solar plexus is the center of self-esteem and honor, it is all about the degree to which a person can honor their truth, keep contracts with themselves, and be in integrity with all aspects of their life. Think about this: For most people it is easier to keep appointments or decisions when these are declared to a witness. Holding to agreements made to yourself, on the other hand, is harder, whether it's about fitness, meditation, or just taking time to do things you love. It's easy to dismiss agreements you make with yourself. Most people are more available to other people than to themselves.

A sacred contract with ourselves means *I mean yes when I say yes and no when I say no. I say I don't know when I don't know.* It means honoring boundaries we set in order to stay healthy and vital, to prevent ourselves from getting drained, and to not live out of obligations or somebody else's expectations.

When people are in alignment, they know it because they have a whole range of emotions that tell them they are in integrity with their own truth. That is, they feel a sense of joy, contentment, peace, and tranquility. When they are out of integrity in terms of acknowledging and honoring their own sacred contracts, they know that too. Third chakra issues come in the form of discontent, frustration, anger, and discomfort. The physical symptoms they produce point toward unresolved issues.

The Inner Adolescent

Blockages in the solar plexus can be traced to adolescence. The old stories, messages, and belief systems that impact how someone operates in life are still at play as they move into adulthood. As the individual steps out of other people's expectations, they are stepping into consciousness. This is when unconscious conflict finally has the opportunity to surface.

This kind of conflict is often a battle between what someone has grown up to believe about themselves and what they really want in life—their life's purpose and essence. It's as if there is a boxing match going on inside. The skilled practitioner can help clients understand what is going on, how to return to the present moment, and how to release old belief systems and stories.

Guiding your practice partners to release their old stories can be as simple as helping them recognize what their true story is in their present moment as an adult. You don't have to go into a whole therapy session about what happened to them when they were ten or fourteen years old, but you can pick up clues that may indicate the starting point of a story that was assimilated because of an expectation or a sense of obligation. When we're kids, we often do what we are told or expected to do, or we integrate the belief systems of our parents and teachers. Those beliefs go into our cellular memory and can come to light in a healing session.

As a practitioner, when you determine that someone has fire and solar plexus issues, you are working to free the inner adolescent on a symbolic level.

What a Blocked or Overactive Solar Plexus Chakra Looks Like

Blockages in the solar plexus might mean a person has poor personal boundaries: someone who can't say no, who constantly needs others' approval and validation because they lack these themselves. They don't honor or believe in themselves, so they have poor self-esteem and a poor sense of trust.

We can get knocked out by what people say to us sometimes. If we have a healthy solar plexus, we know that somebody who says nasty or mean things to us is talking about himself and is projecting those ideas onto us. But if the solar plexus is blocked or weak, the words go right in, we pick them up, and we start feeling badly about ourselves: we believe them. We don't listen to ourselves—in fact, there's not even a self to listen to—and it may take a crisis to get us to act on our own intuition. For example, someone might be unhappy at work and want to leave but not actively pursue a job change—until they get fired for poor performance. Subconsciously, they have created a situation that forces them into another job, but they've done it the hard way. It is important to be able to make changes in our lives without the trauma or drama. And that means listening to ourselves and taking our desires seriously. The solar plexus is the center of willpower, and when it is weak we can remain in a situation that doesn't serve us, in a codependent relationship. Issues of this kind often manifest as a digestive problem, possibly constipation or diarrhea.

Another indication of a blocked solar plexus is a fear of exploring new opportunities, which can come across as aloofness and leads to a sense of isolation.

This quick sketch of solar plexus issues will help you recognize them when they come up. This is really powerful because an understanding of what the solar plexus holds and how this can impact the individual can really aid you in helping your client understand their core issues and verbalize what's going on and set an intention to address it.

When the third chakra is overactive, this can present as being judgmental, quick-tempered, stubborn, and/or positional. There is often a need to control as well as a need to protect oneself through defensiveness.

You can actually see the health of the solar plexus chakra by observing people. Think of how a group of young girls often stands—and more particularly, what they do with their arms. They cross them across their solar plexus. This is absolutely normal for them because they don't know who they are yet, so they are protecting that part of themselves. As a practitioner, be sensitive to cues that present as words and/or behavior.

In your conversations and observations, look for the following indications:

- Keep their word and commitments to themselves
- Need the approval of others
- Have clear boundaries
- Respect the boundaries of others
- Fear empowering others because in doing so, they feel diminished
- Have an energetic reserve
- Listen to their intuition
- Are judgmental of others
- Don't take risks or try new adventures

What an Open and Clear Solar Plexus Looks Like

People with a clear solar plexus take pride in their work and have a strong sense of self-respect and integrity. They say what they do and do what they say, both with themselves and others. They have clear boundaries and rarely attract people who try to put them down or infuse them with negativity. They are in touch with their truth and stand strong without the need to shame or blame others.

When you have a clear solar plexus you have the courage you need in daily life and the ability to turn your thoughts into action. You can also provide selfless service to others because you have good boundaries, so when you agree to do something, you really do want to do it.

Questions for Exploring Solar Plexus Chakra Issues

- What have you not been able to stomach in life, and how is that affecting your physical and/or emotional body?
- In what ways do you sabotage your self-honor?
- How often do you disregard your intuitive voice to please others?
- Do you carry anger or resentment? About what?

If the answers to these questions create grief, sadness, or a sense of loss, they probably relate more to the sacral chakra. If they result in stored anger, bitterness, resentment, or loss of self-worth, it points to the solar plexus.

Also consider that the element of fire can be smoldering (resentment), explosive (rage), or soothing, warm heat. Or perhaps the fire won't burn at all (depletion). You need to consider all of the elements' different facets and nuances in order to be able to know how best to work with them within the sound healing process.

The Solar Plexus Chakra: Doing the Work

Misery loves company but dwelling in it is not an effective way to gain strength or confidence. Since lack of confidence is often a third chakra issue that comes up in clients, you'll do well to move conversations away from energy drains, such as focusing on the wounded part of the self. Instead, steer clients into the present moment. The aim is to put energy into the healthy part of them and keep it there. Keep the perspective on all those things that are working. As I've mentioned before, people tend to judge themselves by their weakest links, taking one small aspect of themselves and superimposing that onto their wholeness, as if it is the totality of who they are.

A skilled practitioner will help the client shift from a self-image of aspects that aren't working and focus on what is working. When we look at what is working, we get revved up and psyched, which gives us energy to keep moving forward. Success is about little tiny positive steps that build on each other.

It's hard to build energy when you're discussing your woes, trauma, trials, and tribulations. All you do is go down, down, down and before you're through, you feel bad about yourself. It's time to change that recording! To help prepare yourself to help your clients, commit to a week in which you will discuss only what is positive and current in your life. Shift your focus from what isn't working, anything that drains your energy, to what works and enhances your energy. Keep a journal to write about your progress.

I realize I haven't even talked about what to do with the instruments yet. That's coming up next, but this is important too. The words that come out of our mouths and are in our heads are often the same. They are all about energy and they affect us and the work we do with the bowls.

The following questions from students offer insights about working with instruments with this chakra.

I worked with a young woman in her twenties, and when I first completed a tingshas diagnosis I felt she had healthy vibrations throughout her body except for her solar plexus—that felt dead. When she was forming the intention, she said she wanted to have more bravery and courage, to be less anxious, so what you are saying about the home of the inner adolescent makes sense here. How can I use fire to help her?

Helping this young woman nourish her fire is important. The ego is often thought of as a bad thing, but that's only partly true. It's bad if ego rules over us, but if we don't have enough ego to stand up for ourselves, we usually become very depressed, sad individuals. You're right about how important it would be to use fire energy to help overcome that. But you also mentioned anxiety, so the first thing is to create a sense of grounding and trust. Bring her into her body with breathing techniques, using the ganta to move anxiety down and out and bowl triads to reduce anxiety levels. When it is time to build energy back up, bring it up from the base to the solar plexus and expand it with spirals, going from the solar plexus outward. You can also bring in supporting bowls from the ears and ankles, all pointing toward the solar plexus. And the auric field visualization is also a wonderful tool to use (see Chapter 18 on affirmation and visualization) to build confidence and self-esteem.

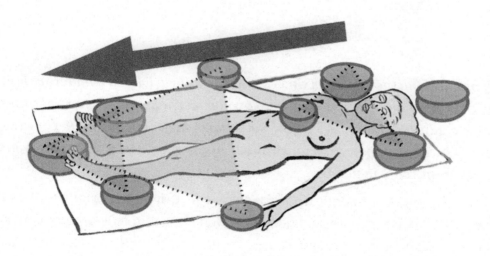

Grounding triads.

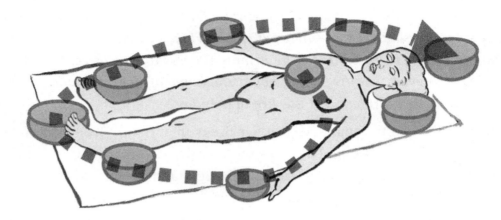

Outward spiral from solar plexus.

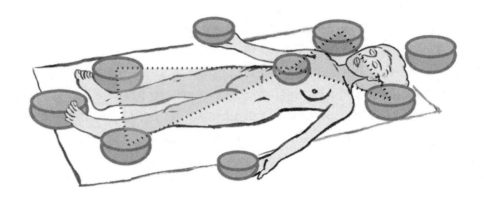

Support from ears and ankles.

My practice partner is an anxious senior in college who is wondering how he is going to make a living. His solar plexus chakra is always the issue and the ganta doesn't ring right. Sometimes his solar plexus is concave, so should I send some fire up through his feet or would that drain his energy from there instead?

Before sending fire energy up through the feet, it is important to create grounding, reduce his stress, and gently sing the ganta to soothe that area. Later you can bring fire and energy right up through the feet and use supporting bowls aimed at the solar plexus.

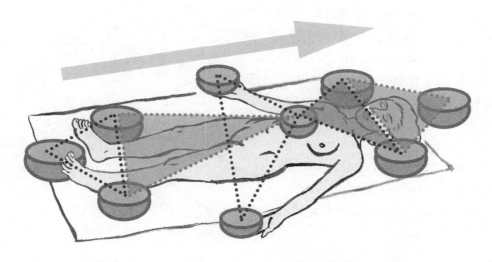

Upward triads bringing fire and supporting bowls.

He sounds quite vulnerable, so be gentle with everything. You always have to neutralize anxiety and stress through grounding and only bring fire back into the body when you can hear alignment in the bowls. Then you can begin the strengthening and expanding process.

People often digress into their "stories." When we're working to bring people into their power, it's important to instead help them stay in the present moment. They're engulfed in what has happened in the past. Or they're afraid about the future—and why worry now about something that may not even happen at all? Releasing past and future stories to come into the present moment is part of building trust in the universe. The more you help people be in the present moment, the more access you gain to attend to the here and now.

The practitioner's job is to utilize words and instruments to bring clients into the safety of the present moment and strengthen the energy from there. When you're working with fire energy issues at the solar plexus, remember that people can be either very depleted or very fired up there. They are two different aspects.

If you're working with someone who has a lot of fire energy, anger, and/ or anxiety, it is important to first release that additional energy through the feet and bring that chakra up into its balanced potential.

As you hold intention for a client, you might silently repeat phrases such as *"I'm grounded in what is true"* and *"I honor my truth"* as you sing or strike the bowls to bring that chakra into its potential. Always use a positive phrase that is associated with a cleared chakra.

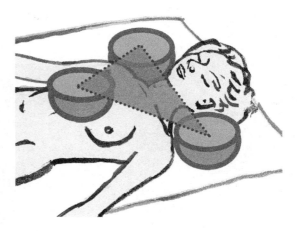

Bowls beside throat.

"I honor my truth" creates an association between the solar plexus and the throat because the center of truth *saying* is the throat chakra. Work with the bowls on either side of the throat (or a bowl held right over the throat) and the solar plexus. Linger on the plexus while singing the bowl, making widening circles over that area.

If the person has a depleted solar plexus, bring the energy of the ground and what is true into the solar plexus by working with the apex of the triad facing up

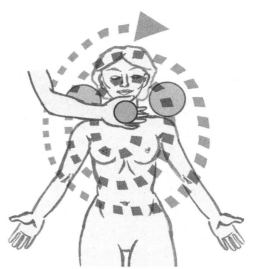

Circles with throat bowl.

and working in an upward direction. (Do this after the initial clearing and grounding.)

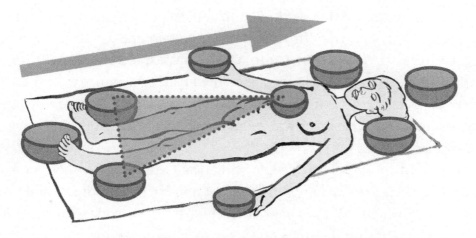

Bringing grounded energy to depleted solar plexus.

Here is an example of bringing in and expanding the power of the solar plexus once it is in alignment:

With the bowl on the solar plexus, sing the bowl clockwise to soothe and then sing the ganta in a clockwise direction to move the energy outward, spiraling from the solar plexus and holding the idea of awareness and expansion of truth. When the solar plexus bowl is resonating well, strike up toward the throat chakra and then between the solar plexus, the heart, and the throat to help them verbalize their truth.

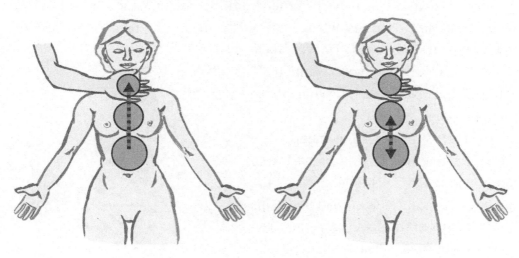

Upward Toward Throat.   *Between Solar Plexus and Heart.*

While performing this work, you may place a dorje vertically between the solar plexus and the throat chakra; these two energy centers are very aligned—they're both about truth. The throat expresses the truth to the world and the solar plexus honors one's own truth. A small crystal dorje fits nicely between bowls. Singing the bowl clockwise to release anxiety and then counterclockwise to reawaken and nourish the fire in the solar plexus also makes sense.

It is great to work with people while they are lying on their stomach since all chakras run along both the front and back sides of the body; you can place bowls on all the chakras on the back and work with them in a similar manner as on the front. In this case, a good metaphor to work with is "getting the monkeys off their back": the things people tolerate that drain their life force.

When you are working on the back, and especially the solar plexus, it is important to establish what those monkeys are:

- Messages that no longer support their well-being
- Other people's expectations that they've been caving in to
- Things in their lives that have lingered and not gotten resolved

The idea is to access past voices and negative belief systems and get the echoes of them off their back. When working on someone's back chakras, you might say, "This is what we're going to do. We're going to get the monkeys off your back. Do you have any monkeys that you want off?" They'll tell you exactly what those monkeys are.

Patterns of sacred geometry are very effective in bringing us back into alignment. For example, using the ganta in a figure-eight pattern helps pull all parts of the person together. You can start it at the heart, solar plexus, throat, or wherever your area of focus

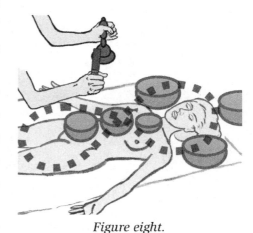

Figure eight.

has been to bring that chakra into the eternal fold. Bring all parts together and then create that sense of flow.

I'm confused about a person's anatomy that may have a concave solar plexus. Can that just be a genetic anatomical part of that person's body, not necessarily meaning that we need to bring fire energy there?

It could be, but I think you will find that the way people stand, sit, and move is often associated with an emotion or an energetic issue. Someone who is concave usually has extreme shyness or feelings of unworthiness that can manifest in a variety of ways.

It might manifest as hiding, timidity, or being critical of others. But it might also show up as an illness. It could just be that the bones were made that way, but nine out of ten times there's something else going on and it's your job to be aware of that. Your tingshas, bowls, and intuition are the tools to help determine what is really at play.

Chapter 12
THE FOURTH OR HEART CHAKRA

Location and Qualities of the Heart Chakra

The fourth chakra, the heart chakra, represents unconditional love and our connection to the divine. It is known to resonate with the notes F or A, so you can work with these notes if you enjoy the Western system of sounding specific notes on the instruments. My preference, as I mentioned earlier, is to work more with tones and harmonics than notes.

The heart is also associated with the color green and two elements—air and water—so consider this when you work with this chakra. Air is very volatile; it can change at any moment. As such, the energy of the heart can very quickly shift from love to hatred, jealousy, and many nuances of emotion. The heart is also about connection. Consider that it is located close to the lungs, which inhale and exhale air that belongs to everyone. The air you're inhaling could be the same air that has gone through trees, ocean life, the Buddha, or even a murderer somewhere. It has probably been around the planet many times before reaching you for this breath. When you exhale you are contributing to a universal pool of air that someone across the oceans, and possibly in different lifetimes, might also inhale or exhale. So the element of air that connects us with everything is associated with the heart.

The ability to expand the universal energy of love, not just outward but also inward to ourselves, is very important in using sound with the heart chakra. Note that the air pathways' long lines travel down our bodies about three-quarters of an inch to each side of the central channel and that the emotion of the air pathway is desire for

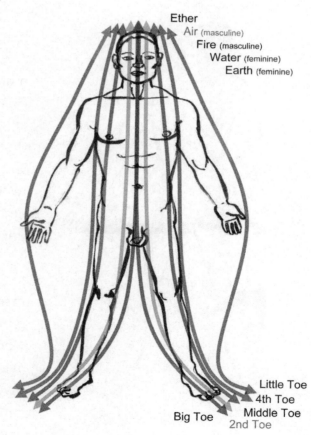

Ether
Air (masculine)
Fire (masculine)
Water (feminine)
Earth (feminine)

Little Toe
4th Toe
Big Toe   Middle Toe
2nd Toe

Elemental long lines.

fulfillment of the spirit. That is another way the heart is associated with the element of air.

The heart is also associated with the element of water, which we find represented in the sacral area and the feet as well. This is the path where we store our very deep sadness, grief, and trauma. Lack of love and nurturing can cause us to create a fragile system of trust and weak sense of self-worth within the sacral chakra, and this can manifest in the heart and impact relationships with people, abundance, and more.

Consider the contrast between the two elements associated with the heart chakra as well. Air is very volatile and changes quickly while water is slower moving, feminine, and flowing in nature.

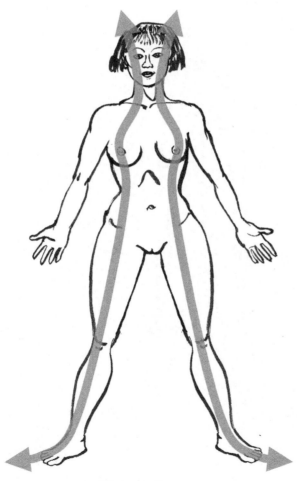

Water pathways.

The heart is the bridge from the lower chakras to the upper chakras, a place of transmutation of energy. It's also the first chakra that connects our external and internal worlds—this is another way in which it is a bridge. It's our connection to the divine within us, our diamond self, and the source of unconditional love.

The heart chakra is linked to our inner teen, so cellular memories from this time period are often present when you work with this chakra. And again, contrasting elements are involved. Remember that water can be slow moving, so these old experiences can circulate in the water pathways of the body for many years. Yet since the heart charka is associated with air as well, it also contains the volatility of those experiences, which could have happened in a split second.

We may not even be conscious of these issues, as is commonly the nature of trauma or grief. Often when we experience pain we just swallow or dismiss it and we don't even recognize how strong a backseat driver it is in our lives. But the foundations of the heart issues and challenges we experience as adults can often be traced to something within that happened in our teenage years, and it manifests over and over again in various ways as we get older. In working with the instruments, we have the opportunity to gain a cognitive association with these old cellular memories and can completely transmute a deep issue, and with that issue, a lot of the peripheral issues around it.

What a Blocked or Overactive Heart Chakra Looks Like

A blocked heart chakra can produce a sense of separation, isolation, lack of emotion, halfheartedness, feelings of being unloved, deep apathy, and a sense that we're only surviving—that we're only a little bit alive. Imagine what it feels like to be a little depressed, with very little joy and not a lot of spark.

A heart broken through deception is one of the biggest energy drains, sapping an enormous amount of life force. Betrayal that resides in the heart chakra is one of the hardest things to heal.

If your heart chakra is blocked and you lack self-love, how can you be open to loving anyone else? This issue is connected to lack of self-worth as well, which can come across as lack of finances or just a "lack of" mentality in general: *I'm not worth it, and I show that I'm not worth it by always having money problems.*

Remember: when we have a blockage in one area, it can manifest in many different ways, but these are the foundational aspects of heart chakra blockage—negative energetic feelings that really deplete the body.

An overactive heart chakra, on the other hand, might manifest as resentment, bigotry, hatred, prejudice, or jealousy.

What an Open and Clear Heart Chakra Looks Like

The energy of forgiveness is the strongest act of self-love, and forgiveness of others entails forgiveness of self. It is not possible to have a clear, open heart while holding on to an issue that requires forgiveness. That would be like trying to release air from a balloon while holding the opening closed. To open and clear our heart chakra, we may need to forgive ourselves for being in a relationship that lacked integrity, for being blind to betrayal, for an angry outburst, or any other actions we have taken that linger in the heart.

With a clear heart chakra there is a sense of harmony: healing power, compassion, attraction and being attractive, being a magnet for manifestation, and the ability to see yourself in others and the best in yourself and others. When the heart chakra is clear, there is a sense that life is flowing and you do not have to trudge through it, and you don't constantly have roadblocks that hinder your sense of flow. Joy and effervescence are aspects of a clear heart chakra.

Questions for Exploring Heart Chakra Issues

- On a scale of 1 to 10 where 1 is lowest, what is your level of self-love?
- What do you most need to forgive in yourself and/or others?
- How connected do you feel to the world and others?
- How would you know that your heart is open?

The Heart Chakra: Doing the Work

If someone comes to you with a broken heart, there's probably some anger there. There's probably some judgment of the other person and of themselves. That's why we can never just work with one chakra. It's very difficult to open up someone's heart if they're holding grief in their sacrum and they have fire energy in their solar plexus.

So you always want to begin by recognizing the peripherals and associations. What other things are going on around this? You know that the heart is most affected right now, but you don't want to expand, contract, or bring in energy there without clearing the other chakras and making room for that shift.

So for example, if I want to work with a broken heart, it may be necessary to first ground angry, fiery energy that lies beneath the surface in the solar plexus, and clear the sadness in the sacrum that originated a long time ago and has been triggered. Only then would it be effective to open and expand the heart energy.

Intense, Heavy Energy in the Heart: The Bowl or the Ganta?

Bowls are generally used for soothing, energizing, aligning, and what I call neutral techniques, which are useful when you are doing visualizations to create an envelope of sound and safety around someone (for example, striking a slow, soft, steady pattern around the head, or a hand-hand-heart pattern, or steadily singing the bowl on the heart). Bowls are not used to break up energy.

Instead, I recommend using the ganta to break up and move blocked heart energy. Remember that to break up energy you gently clack or strike the ganta in a rhythmic pattern, and to soothe you sing it clockwise to release (or expand) energy and counterclockwise to reawaken, strengthen, and nourish, depending on your intention.

In general, in working with the heart chakra respect and gentleness are important, although at times the heart needs a little bit more of an energetic boost. There are many things to keep track of when working with these instruments around the heart. You can strike the bowls in a downward direction for decompression and grounding. You can sing them in a clockwise direction to send energy out (that is, to release it from the person's energy field altogether) or to expand the energy in the heart outward. Be clear in your intention here because even though in both cases you're singing the bowl clockwise, these shifts are distinctly different—you do not want to inadvertently expand energy that you are really aiming to release entirely from the body. Taking care with your intention will help you get the effect you're looking for.

Counterclockwise singing will nourish and strengthen the inner self.

You can use patterns of sacred geometry such as the spiral (inward or outward) to expand or bring in energy or the infinity sign to harmonize different points and create a sense of infinite flow. While there is a variety of approaches, these decisions are not arbitrary; you must select and use them with intention.

The heart is located over the thymus gland, which sends messages to the spleen to produce white blood cells that activate our immune system to keep us healthy, so it is good to activate that gland. There is a simple way to activate your own thymus: make a fist and thump yourself on the thymus. You can do that for your clients by playing a bowl on the heart more energetically in a rhythmic pattern. You can also teach them to thump on their thymus during the day!

Sound healing is a way to help people shift from being victims to being witnesses to their condition. In this way they can more easily open their hearts to their situation and themselves as they progress through their journey while making decisions from a more powerful position.

Breaking Up the "Heart of Stone"

If you perceive a "heart of stone"—a lot of anger or bitterness—it's usually the case that underneath it is hurt. The fear and anger are a reaction, a reflex. They have a protective function, so you need to break up a heart of stone gently. You can break it up a little bit with the ganta by gently clacking it in a rhythmic pattern. And while you're working, work from *your* heart. If you come at it too vigorously, the response is often retreat. If you find fear or anger in the heart, think of working down the chakras. Think relief, bringing the fire energy from the solar plexus back down through the feet to ground it and make space for the heart's expansion. Think about acknowledging and calming first, and then expanding.

In this case it's important to remember to clear the sacrum before working with the heart. An expanded heart is not possible when grief is held in the sacrum because one completely negates the other.

Circles of the Heart

Always refer to the openhearted acceptance of love of self first, because all issues and all illnesses are always pathways and important opportunities for growth. Help your practice partner remember a sense of wholeheartedness. To do this, I like to use the guided visualization that follows, doing so after the person is in a deeply relaxed state; it is one of my favorites and will help your practice partner open their heart to themselves. Be sure to memorize the visualization so you don't sound like you are reading a script. The pace is *very slow* and your voice is *very soft* because your practice partner is in a deeply relaxed state—imagine you are whispering to a sleeping baby. Note that I have added ellipses (...) to indicate strategic pauses. These are important as they give the person time to visualize. This is a perfect time to incorporate the neutral playing technique discussed earlier. That is, singing the bowl on the heart very softly, slowly, and consistently throughout the entire visualization:

> "Please bring into your consciousness ... your perception of a high mountain lake ... so high in clean air. The water is crystalline clear ... so pure ... You stand at its edge and look into the lake. The water is so still you can see your reflection perfectly ... and the little grasses moving at the bottom ...
>
> A stone is thrown in ... creating circles in the water ... each circle touching the next in an ever enlarging pattern ... The circles keep expanding outward ... like the circles of your heart.
>
> The circles of your heart keep getting bigger and bigger ... with you at the center, held fast in love's embrace ... From the outermost edges of the ever-expanding circles you can see yourself through the eyes of love. And this is what you see:
>
> You see all of your gifts, all of your triumphs, your accomplishments and your successes ... All of your

idiosyncrasies, your challenges and failures … You see the totality of every moment of your life combined to create the unique light being that you are … Take a moment to breathe into this … into your heart … acknowledging, appreciating, and accepting who you are, exactly as you are. Stay with that."

At this point you can sing the heart bowl with a bit more rigor, and as the sound gets louder and stronger, say, "Listen to the sound of your heart opening."

Then go on with the session.

A few years ago I was angry after a day of house hunting and took it out on my realtor, who was also my friend. Later I felt guilty for the anger and called to apologize. She said that there was no need for the apology, although I felt there was. She said that I was a "full-spectrum woman." That image was really so wonderful. The ability to embrace our loving self, our wonderful gifts, our inner bitch, and all of who we are is the ability to see ourselves through the eyes of love and look at our full selves, not pushing away any aspect, owning it all, hook, line and sinker, the good, the bad, and the ugly. To be able to feel all that for ourselves and recognize that every part of us is an opportunity for growth and acceptance.

As I mentioned earlier in the book, we cannot release what we don't own. We have to own and accept all parts of ourselves and become more conscious of them. Then, with that consciousness, we can begin to move aspects of ourselves that do not support greater well-being. As we are able to do that for ourselves, we can help our clients do it too. It's really the heart of the whole practice.

We're always a work in progress. But the heart is the foundation of the ability to see ourselves through the eyes of love, to accept ourselves, to see the full spectrum of who we are, and to embrace all of it with a lot of humor. We certainly need that, and as we're able to do that for ourselves, the perspective we gain is a great gift that we can offer to our clients who see themselves as very sick, very angry, or very guilty. All of those qualities are parts of us. Instead of trying to push them away, let's open our hearts to everything we are and take a big sigh of relief in doing it. Then, the heart opens.

Instrument Techniques

There are so many possibilities for working with the heart chakra. I will address some very basic ones, but of course they need to be integrated into the totality of the session. In each case the practitioner needs to determine what the client needs most, but striking in triads that ground challenging energy (such as ear-ear-heart) is a good place to start.

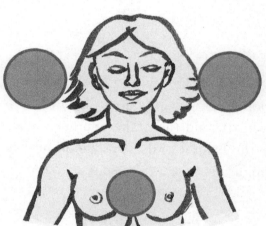

Ear-ear-heart.

Then work more directly on the heart meridian with hand-hand-heart, striking each bowl individually to ascertain that it is reaching its full voice. Hand-hand-heart brings balance via the heart to our masculine and feminine aspects—and thus the mind-body connection.

After working with each bowl individually, strike the bowls as a triad and listen to their collective harmonics to determine that they create a beautiful sound. Then repeat with singing. You can support a dull or weak heart by creating a pattern with the heart center and energizing it with supporting bowls

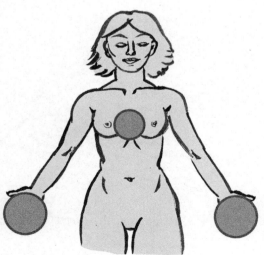

Hand-hand-heart.

(hands and ears to form a kind of star pointing to the heart).

Always clear a chakra first, and then strengthen and expand. In the above-mentioned case, the star pattern strengthens and then you can create an outward spiral pattern—the nautilus—to expand the energy. If the heart contains much anger, take time grounding the anger in downward patterns through the solar plexus and sacrum too, and then use a gentle clanking of the ganta to break up

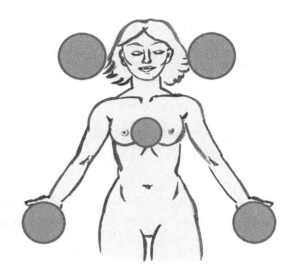

Star pattern.

the energy. When the heart feels clear, make the sign of infinity over it to help balance. We are three-dimensional beings, so you can also create a pattern of hand-hand-heart, ear-ear-heart, and then take another higher-toned bowl and hold it higher over the heart to raise the vibration even further. This forms the pyramid configuration we have discussed before.

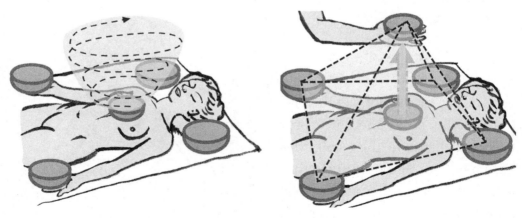

Outward spiral pattern.   *"Pyramid" to raise heart vibration higher.*

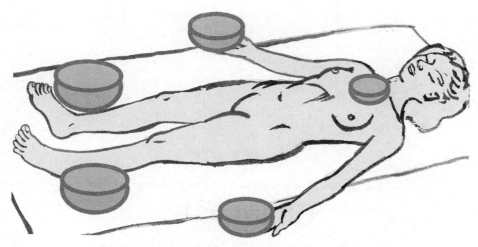

Pattern for a weak heart

If the heart is very weak and needs to remember itself, clear it first and support it with bowls coming in with the heart as the apex from hands and ankles. You can then play counterclockwise spirals with the ganta. The bindi from the dorje can always be used to direct energy right into the heart as well (the bindi, recall, is the sphere in the center of the dorje).

Crossovers are great too (such as ear-heart-hand and hand-heart-ear). This can aid in the communication between the right and left side of the brain and can be helpful when someone is confused, disoriented, or anxious.

The ganta is especially effective at moving, breaking up, and soothing heart energy. There is an interplay with energy moving out and in, and sometimes you need to do both. Remember how strongly associated intention is with everything you're doing. You might work to help the practice partner expand their heart energy and then bring it back into them by creating spirals with the ganta. Then use the bowl to bring that harmony into alignment with the other chakras.

Chapter 13
THE FIFTH OR THROAT CHAKRA

Location and Qualities of the Throat Chakra

The fifth chakra, centered at the throat, often resonates with the note G. It is associated with a mid-blue color. As you can see on the diagram, it is positioned between the heart and the head. Thus this chakra can either help make a strong connection between the heart and the mind or can sabotage any alignment between the two.

When the heart and the mind are aligned, the power to manifest is very strong. Have you noticed how young children are often very good at getting what they want? Their desires are clear and they express themselves directly. Few young children experience a longing for something specific and then talk themselves out of it, thinking they are undeserving, or say they don't want what they actually do want. Yet many adults do exactly that. Let's look at how the throat chakra works for or against us.

The throat chakra is located at the thyroid gland and controls our metabolism, which is a pretty big thing in and of itself: what's centered in the throat impacts the entire energetic system. It also controls the voice and hearing. The fifth chakra reflexes to the pelvis, so the throat and the sacrum are very connected. You would be hard pressed to find someone who is having issues in their sacral chakra who does not also have an issue with expressing their opinions, speaking their truth, or communicating clearly. Insecurity and poor relationships reflect sacral issues and have a high potential to also manifest in the throat.

The throat chakra also reflexes to the feet. Intuitively and symbolically (which is how I most often work), this means that our self-expression is linked to having a good sense of who we are on the earth, whether we stand solidly on the ground or not. The way people stand and walk can tell you an awful lot about their interior life.

One of my students observed that her practice partner had some communication issues, yet the tingshas diagnosis got the biggest reaction from the sacrum, so she worked with that. When she ended the session she asked her practice partner what had been the most significant part of it—and she pointed to her feet and the bowl that was beside them. This is a great example of the reality that many areas of the body are interrelated.

The purpose of the throat chakra is to express what's being perceived by the lower chakras and clear them via sound. When we perceive something, we do not always do so consciously. People who act in fear or live their life in a sense through fear are not saying to themselves, "I'm scared, I'm scared, I'm scared." I don't even think they know that they're responding to life through fear half the time. It's second nature to them—it's just how they are. The practitioner's job is to help them see what is being perceived in a way that is clean, pure, and in the present moment. It is to help them notice when they are in a lot of story and when there is a lot of reactivity and help them clear their chakras so they can express their truth through their words. Remember that words are not always just the words themselves but also how they are expressed. Sound is very blocked in our culture, and when I'm working with a chakra, I can use affirmations that bring that chakra up to its highest potential. A good one for the throat is "I have joy." This holds the space for the person to connect to and express the joy within them.

The Impact of the Throat Chakra

This is the center of divine choice. It is where you take responsibility for your choices by speaking up for yourself and establishing boundaries, by recognizing and honoring your truth through your words. The recognition and honoring of one's truth lives in the solar plexus, but its declaration comes out through the mouth.

Even though another chakra is the center of sacred contracts and self-honoring, the expression of these comes through the throat, whether said silently or aloud. The throat chakra is where you express where you are in relation to the expectations of other people, your society, and your religion, to the extent that these control your life. As you work up from the root and clear the chakras, symbolically you're growing older. Then, when you reach the throat chakra, you enter the present moment. This is the place where you say, "This is it—I'm here now. This is who I am now." It is fully stepping out of living from a sense of obligation and other people's expectations and into your own life.

To borrow a scenario I've mentioned before, self-honoring is expressed at the throat chakra when you're able to finally say, "You would like me to make fifty brownies for the second grade class tomorrow, but that doesn't really work for me right now. What I can do is bring a couple of packages of cookies." When this starts happening, your throat chakra is really working for you. In contrast, when this chakra is blocked you can't express your needs, listen to your inner voice, or control yourself because you are giving your power to others. We give our power away easily, but honoring the self is not just about saying no. It's also about saying yes—when you mean it.

What a Blocked or Overactive Throat Chakra Looks Like

Louise Hay, in her book *You Can Heal Your Life*, mentions that throat issues reflect the inability to see things in a broad manner—a lack of perspective. You know how a duck can twist its head almost all the way around to see things. Having a wide perspective and taking in the perspective of others is an indication of a very clear, clean throat chakra. When someone says, "My way or the highway," it indicates a very blocked chakra. Resistance to change, depression, stubbornness, and choking up are all about preventing the heart's truth from reaching the mind; they are gatekeepers blocking the way.

Along the way up the chakras, the truth must pass through each chakra and especially the heart—that's where the real transmutation begins. Moving this energy through a clear heart chakra keeps lower chakra issues from being expressed in the throat in the form of hard language. Whatever emotions or traumas are stuffed down into the lower chakras have to go through the progression upward, the final and strongest one being through the open heart and then through the throat and out the mouth.

The heart and mind joined together are very powerful and threatening to a weak will. When the heart and the mind are aligned, manifestation happens instantly. You really can't stop the energy from moving extremely fast and powerfully. This alignment is a strong threat to the ego's perceived job of keeping you stuck where you are. A blocked throat chakra is there to act as a saboteur and prevent the alignment of heart and mind.

An overactive throat chakra is completely different from a blocked one. The person will talk a lot and want to dominate any and all conversations. Their way of self-expressing might sound tight, choppy, or brittle, and is often very fast paced. Remember that there's an association with the thyroid too, which means an overactive throat chakra might have elements of a hyperthyroid condition. The person could be hyper, even out of control—there will be lots of energy moving around.

What an Open and Clear Throat Chakra Looks Like

Someone with a clear throat chakra is expressive, has good communication skills, and has the ability to set good, healthy boundaries and take their space. They are able to speak their truth without shaming or blaming others. Calmness is another element of a clear throat chakra. You can often tell how a throat chakra is affected simply by listening to the tone of the voice used; that is key to telling you what is going on.

Another Useful Point

I spent part of a summer with an old friend who has lived alone for a long time. She has never married. She doesn't have a family. If you've ever been with someone who doesn't have an opportunity to have daily conversations with people, do you know what happens? It all comes out: they do not stop talking! It was like I was not even there; only she was, and there was no room for anything but her words. I often look at things symbolically, so I was thinking, *Okay, this is alerting me to how lonely and unseen she feels.* That will certainly contribute to a lack of self-worth.

People who are confident are not afraid of silence. They know that having a mouth doesn't mean it has to be going all the time. The ability to be comfortable with silence when you're around other people is a sign of serenity and can indicate a clear throat chakra.

Questions for Exploring Throat Chakra Issues

Some of the questions you can ask in relation to the throat chakra are:

- In what way might you lie to yourself or others?
- Do you keep your word, and with whom? (Notice people who keep their word with you and those who don't. As for the latter, how do they respond if you hold them accountable?)

- Do you speak your truth?
- Are you often choked up, or have sore throats?
- What do you still need to say and to whom?

These are good questions to ask a practice partner if there are indications of issues with the throat chakra. You may notice people who are constantly clearing their throat or swallowing. Boy, there is an indication that something needs to be said—and they probably don't know what it is.

You might find a person who smokes cigarettes, for instance, or does something else that symbolically numbs their expression (throat). This is a sign of a lack of self-confidence. It is helpful to look at the world symbolically and make these associations with the chakras.

If it seems appropriate, you can ask your practice partner these questions as part of a session addressing fifth chakra blockages:

- Do you feel shame? When? How can you shift this? How can you get your power back? (People who have been really hurt sometimes feel they want to forgive but do not know how express their feelings within themselves or to the other person.)
- How can you get your power back when you feel betrayed or wrong or hurt? (Just a few words are so incredibly strong.)
- How do you express your needs? By asking? Reporting? Whining? Guilt-tripping?

These are the issues we're concerned with when we're doing bowl work with the throat chakra.

Using "I" statements can also work really well when you're clearing the throat chakra (for more on this see Chapter 19 on power language). If someone has a sense of what they need to say, it's great to help them speak their truth this way. These are statements that in no way shame or blame another person. I always give the person an example, something that states what it *feels* like on my end, versus what someone else *did*.

Here's an example I might use. Say someone—your husband or your child—has a pattern of coming in late for dinner, and it really makes you angry. The next time they walk through the door and the food is cold, you say, "You're late again. It really makes me mad." This will immediately put them on the defensive. You're accusing them of being late—and they are—but that's not going to help the situation and will probably lead to an argument.

There's another way to express your truth and your frustration. When they walk in the door you can say, "Hi," and then say something like this: "I'm glad you're here, but it is so frustrating for me when we agree on a time and that's not respected. I try to make a nice dinner and I feel so unappreciated." You will notice that I didn't use the word "you" at all—I didn't make any accusations. Instead I shared with them how that behavior made me feel without any accusing words. The "I" statement is a lot easier for people to hear and they will be more likely to respond with empathy if you use this technique.

If you help your practice partners understand what an "I statement" is and what it's not, that will help them learn to express themselves more effectively.

Choking

Some people will physically choke when you work on this chakra. If this happens you need to stay extremely centered and not get caught up in any feelings of panic—and that's not easy when someone is having a coughing fit. Your reaction will be to try to help them right away, but instead, center, do your breathing, and just hang out with them, letting them do what they need to do. If they have been coughing for quite a long period of time, you might have to reach under them to lift their head. You may also need to remove bowls from their chest so they don't bounce off.

It may help if you make long, slow exhalations on "ahhh." Hearing that centered, audible breath can be calming. If that doesn't work, you can always ask them if they would like something to drink. But resist the temptation to act too quickly. You are holding the space for them to shift things on their own.

Working with the Instruments

The throat is a good place to use the tingshas very gently and softly, to reawaken the voice. There can be so much stuck energy lurking there. Even though you will have already used your tingshas at the beginning of the session for diagnosis, when you get to the throat, it's a place that may need special attention.

One technique with the tingshas is to make larger and larger circles. Strike the pair of tingshas and then let one of them hang down while guiding its direction to make ever widening circles above the throat. Then move on with the ganta and place the dorje vertically on the sternum (and the thymus gland) just below the throat and between the heart and the throat.

Work with your intention, directing the heart energy right up through the dorje and very gently doing some ganta work, such as striking in a gentle, rhythmic pattern to energize the connection or singing gently either clockwise or counterclockwise, depending on what is needed. If the person is doing a lot of coughing, you might want to do some very, very gentle clacking to break up the constriction. But mostly you will want to sing it very gently and make releasing clockwise spirals.

I never place a bowl directly on the throat (or the third eye)—this is a very sensitive area of the body. I think it is best to work just above the throat or barely touching it. I have a very small, very lightweight crystal that I put on the throat, and a little tiny dorje crystal that I put on the third eye, but those are the only things I ever place there and I do it to magnify the work.

If someone has a very long throat and I can access it (sometimes there just isn't room), I usually put the bowl in my hand and then very gently lay the backs of a couple of my fingers on the throat so they can feel the vibrations. But it's got to be a very light, feather touch.

In terms of configuration of the instruments, here are a few options that can be effective for the throat, bearing in mind the interconnections of the chakras and the reflexes in the feet. You could do throat-sacral-foot to clear the chakras that are in association. You could also do ankle-ankle-throat to create a sense of stability that you then bring up to the throat. Once the sacrum is clear you can alternate between the throat and sacrum, listening for a beautiful, harmonious sound. You can also place bowls on either side of the clear sacrum and hold one over the throat to strengthen the accord between them. Remember that the throat is always going to be an apex. If you are working your way down the body, you can use ear-ear-throat, then a straight line from crown-throat-sacrum-foot. If you are working with someone with hyperactivity issues, remember to bring energy downward toward the feet with the triads. Alternatively, if you want to create a balancing pattern, you can do throat-throat-grounding bowl, then ankle-ankle-throat to make a star shape. (Remember to hold the bowl just above the throat, not directly on it.)

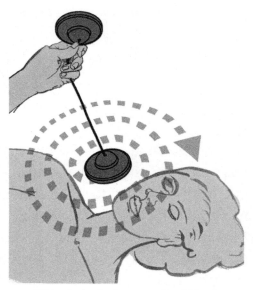

Tingshas circles over the throat.

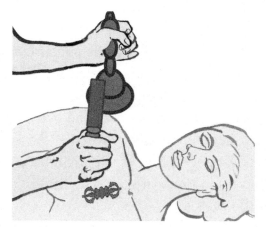

Ganta with Dorje on sternum.

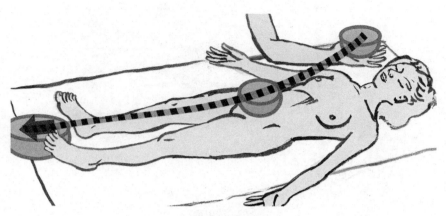

Throat-sacral-foot.

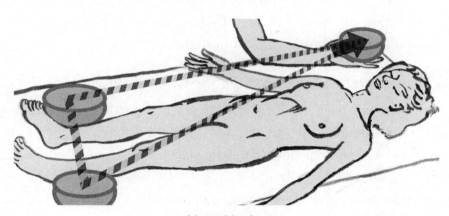

Ankle-ankle-throat.

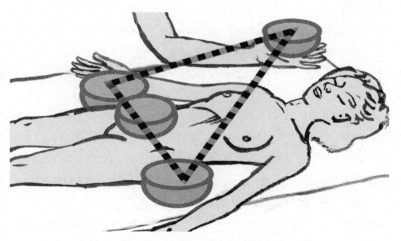

Bowls on each side of cleared sacrum.

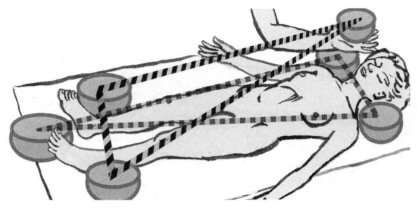

Star shape.

The star pattern works wonderfully for hyperactivity because it is the perfect balance of masculine and feminine energy.

Strengthening and Energizing, from the Ground Up

Let's say you have been working with a practice partner and you want to strengthen and energize from the ground up, right through the heart and out of the mouth. You've done some "I statements" and created the intention "I communicate my truth clearly and simply." Now you need to find a way to bring up some energy and strengthen that intention. An effective way to do this would be to work from the root and go straight up the chakras into the throat. You could stabilize that with an ankle-ankle-throat triad. The intention here is to bring the sense of confidence, strength, and stability from Mother Earth right up the person's system. Visualizations focused on associating the heart and throat (connecting to truth and expressing it) can be very effective as well.

You've probably noticed by now that the patterns you use can be very similar from one chakra to the next. You need to understand the principles and patterns to use in order to create certain energetic imprints such as balancing patterns, energizing patterns, soothing patterns, strengthening patterns, expanding patterns, and nourishing patterns (triads, circles, the infinity sign, spirals, and direction of flow). Listen to the instruments and correct any dis-harmonies or weak-voiced bowls.

Chapter 14

THE SIXTH OR THIRD EYE AND
SEVENTH OR CROWN CHAKRAS

I am combining the discussion on working with these two last chakras in part because they are located so close together in the body. Also, by now, you will be familiar with the basic principles of chakra work so I can be a little briefer here.

Location and Qualities of the Third Eye Chakra

The third eye is located directly between the eyebrows and is associated with the color purple. It is a delicate chakra to work on and is deeply connected to the kundalini energy stored in the root chakra. When we work with the third eye we want a clear and pure line of energy to come up the body in a directed manner. If the chakra points in between are not cleared first, we will invite an explosion of energy—exactly what we don't want. So before you bring your attention here, make sure you clear the central channel. In this way you are clearing energies that start at the physical level and work up into the more spiritual realms.

The element of the third eye is ether. Its note is A. The third eye is a seed of consciousness, inspiration, knowing, mindfulness, and acknowledgment. It connects with our intuition. It also works with the immune system and the pituitary gland, which stimulates the thyroid to clear mental traffic jams. This is important in helping dismantle the rational mind in order to allow the spiritual journey to unfold. (Have you ever noticed that when your mind becomes overwhelmed, you want to drop everything and just take a walk and ground yourself? The impulse to clear mental traffic jams is natural, and the third eye is important in doing this.)

Remember that those of us who work with the bowls understand that everything is interconnected, all the chakras are related, and it is not effective to work with one chakra out of context. While we want to work on overactivity in the third eye, we must remember reflex points and indirect ways to access to that chakra.

What a Blocked or Overactive Third Eye Chakra Looks Like

A blocked third eye might manifest as a lack of imagination or creative energy. It can present as worry, forgetfulness, confusion, or being closed to a sense of vision or higher perceptions (which can also indicate blockage in the root chakra). For example, one might have tunnel vision about a situation, staying focused on its mundane, physical, and survival-oriented aspects rather than having a broad range of options and perceptions about it. If a strong attachment to this attitude presents itself, it might also indicate that the throat chakra is involved. (A blocked throat can indicate an inability to take in other people's views: a positional mind-set.)

Attention deficit disorder (ADD) could indicate an overactive third eye chakra. Picking up on and taking in everything around oneself is another. This leads to mental exhaustion and oversensitivity, chaos in the mind, jumping to conclusions, and paranoia.

What an Open and Clear Third Eye Chakra Looks Like

A clear third eye creates confidence in one's intuition, the ability to see what to do in a situation and choose appropriate action, and a commitment to one's higher self. An active imagination, creativity, and a connection to spiritual things also indicate clarity.

Once when I was conducting a workshop for cancer clients, I guided them in a meditation that offered a heightened, expansive, positive vision of themselves—a vision of wellness. Then I appealed to their inner healer and reminded them that creating a higher vibration meant connecting with this vision. This is very healing. These inspired words came to me because I was able to stimulate and clear my third eye. Most attendees had a strong, effective experience, although some got stuck and couldn't visualize everything. If time had permitted, I would have been able to do some personal work with those people to help clear their third eye and unleash the confidence in their intuition that would help them access their intuition and imagination.

Questions to Explore for Third Eye Chakra Issues

Consider the following questions related to the third eye chakra, a valuable inquiry whether you're working with yourself or with your practice partners. Notice patterns of speech and the kinds of statements that might indicate whether the third eye is clear or not:

- Are your decisions mostly based on details and rational procedures or on hunches?

- What, if any, is your connection to a higher power?
- What is your relationship with your creative energy?
- Are you able to see things from several perspectives?

Spiritual growth is marked by the ability to get the mind to be okay with seemingly irrational choices, and intuition is the ability to know without having a rational explanation. Discernment is important in making choices, as it would be foolish to act based only on a hunch. But getting a sense of your or your practice partner's tendencies in these three areas will help you in working with this chakra.

On Intuition

Consider how you perceive your intuition and how it comes forward for you. Many people, when their intuition is on to something, experience an inkling or a sensation in their stomach or solar plexus. When their intuition is really on target, people often feel a little flood of warm, prickly heat; think about the times when you have felt that for yourself. Others see images or hear words. And if none of these seem to apply to you, be aware of what goes on in your body when you get a hunch or a moment of intuition and then pay attention to it and learn to trust it.

So what about a definite intuitive "no"? A "This is not right"? This may come across as a "bad" feeling in the stomach.

One of my students described their intuitive no as "nervous blood": a thought unaccompanied by words that feels something like thirst or hunger. It takes some time and attention to develop the ability to recognize how your intuition comes to you, how you experience "knowingness." During a session it is important to let the sound and sound healing principles guide you, but intuition and a clear third eye chakra are equally important—because one day you will be standing over a client and you might not have a clue about what to do. When that happens, you have a choice to either tune in to your intuition and really let it guide you or go into "Okay, I'll just strike that bowl and hope it does something" mode: not ideal. You want your intuition to be available to you as a resource as much as possible.

If you're not tuned in to your intuition, a sound healing session can become very frightening. But if you can access it, there is a beautiful flow: you know exactly what to do and it feels good to be able to be practicing— you feel grounded and confident. This happens more and more when you have internalized the principles of sound healing so well that they are second nature.

The first time I received a very strong message about my intuition and how to trust it was when I was offering a polarity therapy session. I was working on a client's abdomen when I had a piercing feeling in my gut. I didn't know whether I was making it up or not, but I just stayed with that feeling and started soothing that area on my client. After the session I shared my experience with her. She told me she had been raped by her brother, and that's where the pain was living. She had never spoken of it to anyone or been able to release it before that day.

I learned from that experience. I get my intuition in many ways, including through my body as I did that day. Sometimes I physically feel what is going on with the client in my own body, sometimes an image appears, and sometimes I just know. A clear third eye will help you not only receive your intuition, but really become rooted and confident in it.

The Third Eye Chakra: Doing the Work

The best object to place directly on the third eye is a tiny crystal dorje because light goes through it and crystal is a conductor of energy. Another material might feel like you're putting a lid on the third eye, actually obstructing instead of clearing it. However, if your practice partner is on their stomach with their head in a headrest, you can place a bowl on the back of the head over the third eye and strike it very gently in a rhythmic manner to wake up this chakra.

Other layouts create a pyramid; that is, you float a bowl in your hand above the third eye, adding a third dimension.

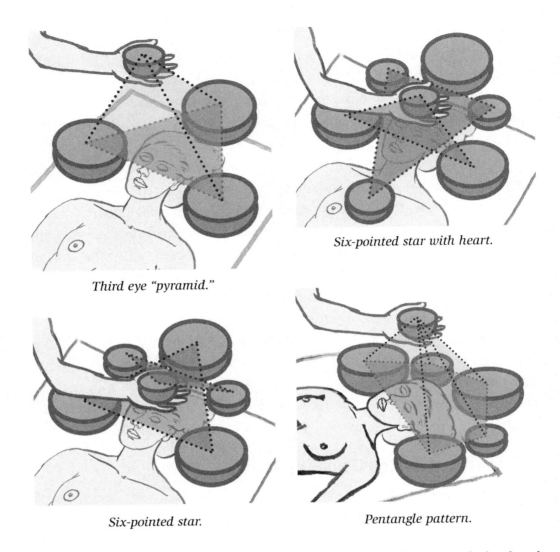

Third eye "pyramid."

Six-pointed star with heart.

Six-pointed star.

Pentangle pattern.

You can create a kind of rainbow with five bowls around the head stretching from ear to ear. Place a bowl between the crown and the ear on either side of the head—let's call those two bowls mid-bowls. They should have lovely harmonious tones with the other bowls around the head. Then, holding the bowl above the third eye, play mid-bowl-mid-bowl-third eye as one triad, and ear-ear-crown as the second triad. This configuration forms a six-pointed star.

Another triad that connects the third eye and the heart is ear-ear-third eye (using a floater bowl above the third eye) as the first triad, then mid-bowl-mid-bowl-heart as the second triad, again forming a six-pointed star. When striking the third eye floater bowl, you can make spiraling motions in a clockwise direction, starting very small and expanding outward (or vice versa to bring the energy of the third eye inward).

A third eye bowl is normally quite small and high pitched, with a clear, pure sound. Toward the end of a session, when appropriate, you can start about three feet above the head and strike it, then bring it down toward the third eye while making spirals.

These three-dimensional patterns are great, but if you are trying something new it is a good idea to try it on yourself first. Putting a bowl or a crystal on your third eye, front or back, can create an intense feeling. It is good to experience that before you do it for someone else.

Location and Qualities of the Crown Chakra

The seventh or crown chakra is located just above the central part of the top of the head. It is represented by the white light above the figure's head on the diagram at the start of this chapter. The representative note is considered to be B, and it is associated with the central nervous system, brain, right eye, and pineal gland (which regulates the production of melatonin, linked to our internal clock).

The crown chakra is the center of spirituality, dynamic thought, and energy. It is the receptor for the flow of wisdom and cosmic consciousness, and is the place where it is said that the soul enters and exits the body. This chakra is completely connected to the balance of the other six chakras.

What a Blocked or Overactive Crown Chakra Looks Like

Characteristics of a blocked crown chakra could include being spiritually unaware and uninspired, with a constant sense of frustration and separation coupled with deep fatigue. It may also show up as a lack of purpose, and challenges with learning and making decisions. It can cause headaches and poor memory, vision, and coordination.

An overactive crown chakra is ungrounded, with the person ignoring their physical needs. They can also be overly rigid in their thinking and challenged in communication, which can cause confusion, leading to spiritual addiction and depression and a general malaise in self-expression.

When identifying issues that may relate to the crown chakra, consider whether:

- Thoughts and behaviors have repetitive patterns, and life issues linger
- The person identifies more with what they do and have than with a sense of essence
- There is a constant struggle to stay in control of most situations
- There is the ability to tune in to a higher power
- There is acceptance and love of self

What a Clear Crown Chakra Looks Like

Someone with a clear crown chakra is spiritually conscious and connected to the divine and the higher self. They feel a sense of oneness in the universe and have an open-minded attitude. A healthy nervous system contributes to being able to see the wisdom and gifts in any situation, being at peace with self, and having inspired thoughts and an inspired life.

Questions for Exploring Crown Chakra Issues

What kinds of things do you think about every day?

Do you know how to "let go"? Are you comfortable with that?

When and how do you "tune in" to your higher power?

Do you have a sense of yourself as an energetic being?

The Crown Chakra: Doing the Work

After the other chakras are clear and aligned, you might work with one bowl above the crown, creating an expanding nautilus in a clockwise direction to open and strengthen.

Working the ear-ear-crown triad from lowest to highest would be effective to reawaken and energize the crown as well. Another possibility is to float a higher-pitched bowl above the crown bowl and play ear-ear-crown, above the crown, sending the energy away from the body to expand the energy of that chakra even more.

If the chakra is blocked, any of the preceding techniques would work well after some gentle clanking of the ganta. Then you can sing the crown bowl counterclockwise while offering an affirmation.

What else would make sense using the techniques you know by now? That's right: affirmations. Use these to invite connectedness to body and spirit as well as a sense of oneness with the universe, and to provide inspiration. Create affirmations that either strengthen a positive aspect or resolve a challenge. Here are three to try:

- I am connected to the Source of all knowledge and creativity.
- I am connected to my unique, radiant, and loving essence.
- I live my life from a place of love and contentment.

At the end of a session where you have worked with the crown chakra, it is good to offer homework that energizes the characteristics of the crown chakra. This could mean meditation, random acts of kindness, or . . . This is a perfect place for you to be inspired and creative!

Part IV

Working with Challenging Emotions

This section of the book is a short but important one. It focuses on two kinds of energetic imbalance that your practice partners and clients may be concerned about: anxiety and depression. Both are very common—everyone experiences them, at least from time to time. So let's spend a little time exploring how to address them with sound healing.

Chapter 15

WORKING WITH ANXIETY

What Is Anxiety?

The *Oxford English Dictionary* defines anxiety as "A feeling of worry, nervousness, or unease, typically about an imminent event or something with an uncertain outcome."

My definition of anxiety is this: a physiological state characterized by cognitive, emotional, and behavioral components that combine to create the feelings that we typically recognize as fear, dread, panic, and claustrophobia.

Physical sensations that commonly accompany anxiety can include:

- Heart palpitations
- Nausea
- Chills
- Clammy hands
- The need to pee
- Sweating
- Trembling

- Headaches
- Increased blood pressure and heart rate
- Immune system inhibition
- An expectation of uncertain danger, that something is lurking, that something could possibly happen that's not going to be good

As the body prepares to deal with a perceived threat, the tendency is to escape or avoid the source of the anxiety. This is a time of high sensitivity. You can use sound to smooth the circulation of overly sensitive energy. This necessitates using a gentle touch to establish trust and lull the client into a state of openness so they can receive the treatment. It is important to avoid anything that could be startling. You can use a soft voice, long, slow exhalations, and the instruments to help the client shift from fear of the future to experiencing the present moment.

There are many methods to start this process using breath. When the practitioner's breath is slow, with long, comfortable exhalations, this helps the client slow down as well. When you hear somebody breathing really fast, what do you notice about your own heartbeat and your own state? You pick up on that, and your heartbeat may increase; you may feel anxious too. This is entrainment, and you have to be well grounded and able to maintain a high vibratory state to stay in your body and not be swayed by someone else's vibration.

The first thing you want to do for someone who is anxious is to get them out of their head (their story, their self-chatter) and into their body. A person who is anxious is not really inhabiting their body. Instead, their body is in reaction to what's going on with their story, whatever that may be. In other words, their physical state is a response to and manifestation of their story.

A good way to help your practice partner start reinhabiting their body is to ask them to take deep, very slow breaths and focus on long, slow exhalations while saying "Ahhh." Also ask them to follow the journey of the breath in their body with their consciousness—to rest their attention on the breath.

Why "Ahhh"? It's the sound of the heart opening, and any emotion, any feeling, can release into the ocean of love energy. That begins the process. Use breath (and toning, if you wish) to decompress, release anxiety, and start bringing them into a relaxed, safe state of being. Gentle hands-on work is also a good way to create a sense of safety and comfort. The hands-on Presencing process is a way to feel someone's energy and introduce them to yours in a session.

Occipital hold.

To engage the relaxation response, begin by placing your hands under the occipital bone. Hold this position for a minute or two until the client makes a deep sigh. At this point you can quietly repeat the intention you are working with for the session.

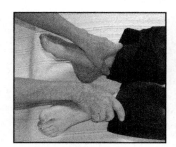
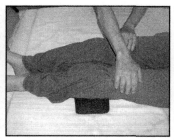
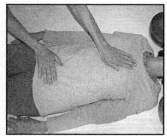

Hands on Ankles.   *Hands on Knees.*   *Hands on Chest and Stomach.*

Gently releasing the head, you can then place your hands on the client's shoulders and push down softly. Then go to the feet and place your hands on the ankles, then the knees, the lower abdomen, solar plexus, heart, and finally one finger on the third eye chakra and then the crown chakra.

Although this sequence seems quite simple, it is not as easy as it looks, and there are many things to pay attention to along the way:

Start by checking yourself. Close your eyes. Take a moment, a breath or two, and center yourself. Be comfortable with the silence. The following process can take about five minutes. Work your way up the body from ankles to head in the following manner. (Note: Placing hands requires very little or no pressure.) Make sure one hand is always on the body as you move from one area to the next—you want to maintain contact throughout. This means you will place one hand first, then the next.

- Make sure your hands are warm, and then place your hands gently and lightly on the client's ankles without pressing down. Just allow them to be there and keep centered, with a steady breath. Watch the client for signs such as a shift in breathing.
- Next, place your hands on the client's knees. Again, watch for signs of relaxation.
- Place your right hand in between client's thighs about a hand's length down the thigh, palm facing the root chakra. Place your left hand on the abdomen below the navel.
- Place your right hand on the abdomen below the navel and your left hand on the heart.
- Place your right hand on the heart and your left hand on the throat.
- Place your right hand on the throat and your index finger of your left hand on the third eye.
- Finally, place your index finger of your right hand on the third eye and your left hand on the crown chakra.

Someone who is feeling anxious can also easily feel trapped. Placing bowls in their hands may especially cause them to feel confined. Often anxiety causes a need to scratch; it's as if the whole body is itching. And people often move their hands to help dissipate anxiety. So if you suddenly place two bowls in their hands, be aware that this could increase their anxiety. Something similar may happen with the eyes, as many anxious people feel unsafe if their eyes are covered with an eye pillow, something I often do. When you have a client who is anxious and you know this, you may have to talk and breathe them down into a state of calmness.

If you are ready to put the bowls on your practice partner's hands, you might start by bringing the energy down to their feet. Then say, "I'm going to put some bowls in your hands. Please exhale with me and allow this. If you feel tension coming up, breathe it out on 'ahhh.' Breathe and allow, breathe and allow. If it gets uncomfortable, all you have to do is say something and I'll remove them."

The idea is to remove obstacles ahead of time so they don't feel trapped and unable to defend themselves. If you address the fear of feeling physically trapped, they will know that if they do feel anxious, it will be okay, and that they have the option of removing the bowls from their hands.

Another thing that can be frightening to someone experiencing anxiety, especially in the beginning, is silence; that's because if you are silent, they can go straight back into the story that has created anxiety. In this case, you can "talk them down" into relaxation, speaking slowly and letting your volume fade as you watch their breath and notice little twitching or eye movements. You might say something like "There will be brief silences as I move the energy in your body. Please use this time to focus on your breath and invite even more letting go." Then work to move the energy down toward the feet, away from the head, grounding into the present moment.

Giving your practice partner grounding techniques to do between sessions is also part of working with them. This is where you can use your creativity. For example, you could suggest they do "releasing breaths" when they feel anxious (inhaling through the nose and long exhalations through the mouth) or "relaxing breaths" (in and out through the nose, again with long exhalations). Or suggest they walk barefoot in water or on sand, or do a yoga movement that brings them out of their head and into their body.

Where Does Anxiety Live, More Often Than Not?

When I ask this of my students, I get responses such as the head, the mind, the stomach, and the solar plexus. But really—anxiety lives in the future. The source of anxiety is the fear that something bad or frightening is going to happen. Yet anxiety is *stored* in the stomach, the head, and the solar plexus. What about the temperature of anxiety? That can sometimes be hard to work out. Is it hot or is it cold? Or does it depend? One way people manifest anxiety is by having both cold and sweaty palms. Anxiety can mean revving up heat or shutting down completely—freezing.

If the anxiety manifests as heat, it needs to be gently smoothed out and cooled down. If it shows up as freezing, it needs thawing out and gentle re-energizing. You can see how important it is to notice how the anxiety is manifesting so you can choose effective ways of working with it.

Instrument Techniques for Neutralizing Anxiety

I suggest you use deeper tones, especially around the head. Work very slowly and give your client plenty of time between patterns and between singing individual bowls (singing is more soothing than striking the bowls when done correctly). Move the energy from crown to feet. Intend that you are drawing a person into peacefulness. You might start the work very quietly so the person has to listen carefully to hear, slowly raising the volume and pace as a way to ease them out of their anxiety.

You know that the apex of a triad can be on top (closer to the head) or on the bottom (closer to the feet), right? When you're working with anxiety, you want to work with bringing the patterns down—the apex toward the feet—to ground and soothe. No quick changes in volume, no quick changes in tempo, and nothing that could be experienced as a pounding.

Create downward triads.

Note that repeating a pattern might feel like pounding if it's done too fast and too loud. Yet repeating a pattern is important. Someone who is anxious needs something to hold on to, and a pattern lends a sense of familiarity. The anchoring pattern around the head creates that sense of safety, but only when it is played slowly and softly and repeated regularly.

There are other ways to work that will help get the mind off the mind! Try this yourself right now, and then you can use it with practice partners. Close your eyes and visualize a beautiful cooling color. Breathe it in and down your central channel, filling all the veins and capillaries along the way. Allow yourself to become that color. Just let yourself experience the texture of the color, all aspects of that color. It's in you … it's emanating from you. A lot of people visualize blues, greens, and turquoise.

If you take your time with this, you should become very relaxed, and this simple visualization can bring your partner into present moment. It's a way to distract them from what they're fixated on.

Be aware that you can't get rid of anxiety directly. You can't say, "Okay, I want you to change your mind, I want you to stop being anxious." You have to keep tantalizing your partner with your voice, with the instruments, and with cool little things such as this visualization that will help them get out of story. With time, they will get a little bit more relaxed. You will see it in their face and in their breath.

Moving energy through the feet and working that foot bowl away from the body is helpful too, so make sure you put that bowl close enough to the person's feet that they can feel the vibration. Then send the vibration out, away from the body. If you have three bowls you can also form the foot triad (ankle-ankle-foot), making sure to play the bottom bowl (foot) away from the body and that it is the lowest tone of the three.

When you strike a bowl with one hand, put your other hand near the bowl, and then move your hand back, you can sense where you stop feeling the vibration. Make sure that the foot bowl is within the range where your partner will feel its vibration.

People with anxiety often lack a sense of a supportive base. After you ground their anxiety by playing downward patterns, then you can start to create patterns of support. One of my favorite balancing and supportive patterns is the star (ankle-ankle-crown and ear-ear-foot) a configuration of two triangles like the Star of David.

Anxious people also want a sense of protection, and you can create a membrane of protective energy all around them by walking in a circle, starting at the feet and circling in a clockwise direction while singing a lower-toned bowl above them. After a few sessions, when they have become more centered, calm, and strong, you can strike all the bowls so they feel themselves at the very center of that circle of sound with the hum of vibration all around them. Remember that when you're doing this, there's a tendency to get louder and faster, so be very careful around their heads, as this is a place you will return to again and again.

You definitely don't want to do something that will wake the person up. You want to keep them in a sound stupor, creating the familiarity of sound but not overdoing it to the point where it feels like a pounding, which will be very uncomfortable. This is something that requires practice—you have to be able to feel out the best pace and volume.

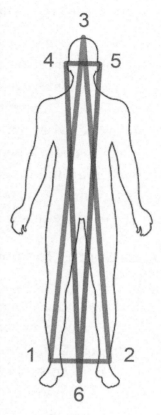

Star pattern.

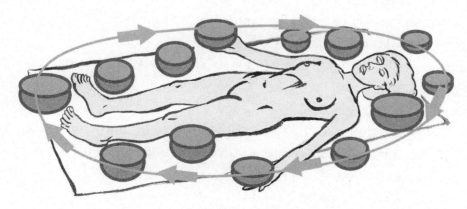

Clockwise circle with bowls.

Clockwise or Counterclockwise?

This depends on your intention. Start with clockwise movement and the intention of releasing the anxiety in a soothing way. If the area you're working becomes clear and balanced and you want to reawaken the innate energy that has been distorted by anxiety, then you can play counterclockwise, but only after the energy is balanced and the anxiety has dissipated. When you play counterclockwise, you are actually reawakening the innate energy, rather than "bringing in" energy. The energy is already there but has been distorted, dormant, and disconnected from the whole in some way.

Case Studies to Ponder

A woman I'll call Ms. X came in with a severe anxiety disorder and a bowl of food. She explained that she felt the need to eat a few bites every few minutes.

How would you handle this situation? Here's what I did.

First of all, explain that this session is for her, and if she needs to eat, it is okay to do so. In fact, it represents a major disruption of the session, but giving her permission to do this allows her to feel safe and have some control. If instead you say, "Oh, that's not possible. It will disrupt the treatment," you will create even more anxiety for her, rendering her unable to act out her behavior. Remove the obstacles by aligning with her needs so there is nothing she needs to defend against. As soon as she feels like she can eat if she wants to, what do you think will happen? That's right. She won't need to do it as much.

This particular woman came in for six sessions. When she did it the first time, I said, "Okay, you just let me know when, and I'll take the bowls off." The first session, she got up to eat a few bites four times, the second time she did it twice, and after that she didn't need to do it anymore. In a case like this, it's important to create a space where the person feels safe and accepted, and not judged.

This case called for talking her down. I don't mean doing a lot of talking; I mean using your voice very gently to slow things down, softening your voice and getting into the breath. As you are doing it yourself, they will entrain with your calm energy. You definitely don't want to entrain with theirs! The trick is to do it so progressively that they don't even know it's happening.

Here are some other ways to soothe this person and help reduce her anxiety:

You might put a small- to medium-size bowl right on the solar plexus and sing it gently for a little while. I have a little pillow with uncooked rice in it that I can warm up in the microwave and I can also place that. I put it on her feet to bring the energy down and create that warm cozy feeling that is easy to relax into—even though we're cooling the energy of anxiety.

So allowing this woman to get up and eat, do whatever she needed to do, just listening to her, being there for her, helped her get into present moment. She eats because she's anxious, and you continue to bring her back to now through repetition. "Okay, now let's do some breathing, and bring you back into present moment. Let's lie you back down. Okay, let's keep breathing into present moment." You may even talk to her while singing a bowl, just talking her down, playing the bowl on the solar plexus while in a whisper, saying, "And now stay with your breathing, stay with your breathing and feel how soothing this is … feel the vibrations throughout your entire body and how wonderful that feels," slowly letting your voice drift off and then continuing to work with the instruments.

Another person—I'll call him Mr. Y—warned me on the phone ahead of time that he was taking a medication that caused him to have to get up and pee all the time. He had a lot of embarrassment and anxiety about that. Plus, he didn't want bowls in his hands or an eye pillow. I had to be quite sensitive about what might feel restrictive to him but would still allow me to work effectively. I did not place a bowl on his sacrum because that would just stimulate the part of him where he was already very anxious. I simply held the bowl *over* the sacrum to gently sing it when I got to that area. His body would know it, but his brain would probably not react with more anxiety. So this was yet another way to diminish anxiety yet still do what I felt I needed to do.

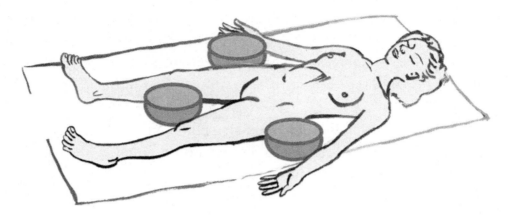

Hip-root triad.

If there is a good amount of trust between you and your practice partner, you could also put bowls on either side of the sacrum and have them spread their legs enough for you to place a bowl near their root chakra. If you're working with someone who has anxiety and by the fourth session you have them lying down spread-eagled with a bowl right in their groin, that is a real accomplishment and a sign they have gone into a place of trust.

Chapter 16

WORKING WITH DEPRESSION

About Depression

Most of us have experienced some form of depression that produces a downturn in mood. This may be relatively transitory and perhaps in response to something trivial. Then there is clinical depression, which the Mayo Clinic defines as "a mood disorder that causes a persistent feeling of sadness and loss of interest." This type of depression can last for several weeks or more and is severe enough to interfere with people's daily lives.

I have found clinical depression to be one of the most challenging situations to work with because it is so far reaching. People who are depressed are in a very fragile state because depression is a volatile energy, and it can range from overwhelming—where someone is completely in their head—to hopeless, perhaps a result of trauma or the death of a loved one, leaving them empty and isolated. In my experience, clients with depression have the least energy available to partner with me in their healing; they just want to come in and be fixed. But healing is absolutely a partnership, and it is a challenge to get buy-in from someone who is suffering from depression.

Depression, sadness, hopelessness, discouragement, down in the dumps: these are all states that often come about as a result of physical exhaustion, a traumatic event, or a chemical or hormonal imbalance. Depression is earth energy (think of dense clay) that moves very slowly. In order to decide how best to approach this problem, it is important to determine what the client is already doing nutritionally, what's going on in their relationships, whether they're on medication, and how much exercise they get. The information they provide and the answers to those questions will inform what you do.

If someone is suffering from physical exhaustion, your protocol will be different from what you choose if they're in shock as a result of a traumatic event or a chemical imbalance. Having "the blues" from three days of travel is different from undergoing the loss of a loved one or a divorce. And by the way, no matter what the source of the problem is or how it is manifesting, be sure you have a support team you can refer clients to, including a therapist, nutritionist, physician, and physical trainer.

Loss of energy and motivation is a big factor with depression. Getting the energy moving again to help the client reconnect with their sense of joy and hope is going to be part of your session, after breaking up and grounding the stuckness you find.

After the initial tingshas diagnosis to wake up the dormant energies and indicate where blockages or overactivity are present, you can use the ganta and dorje to help break up stuckness and ground the energy of all the chakras. Because depression locates itself in the root and sacrum and is associated with earth energy, those areas should get extra attention. Integrating work with the solar plexus and heart, both individually and in connection to each other, using the dorje and the ganta with the infinity pattern is also important because, as you know, all the chakras are connected. For example, heartbreak can be the catalyst for depression.

Blocked earth energy is slow moving, so it can take many sessions to make a shift. Be patient. The solar plexus is the center of will, and some fire energy can get things moving again there. Creating an energizing rhythmic pattern above the solar plexus with the ganta can be effective for this. And if a sense of hopelessness or disheartenment is present, you can gently soothe that by singing the ganta in a clockwise direction and then striking in a more energizing pattern in a counterclockwise direction to nourish the heart.

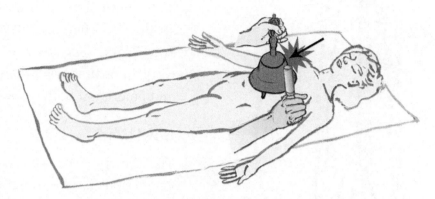

Strike ganta above heart.

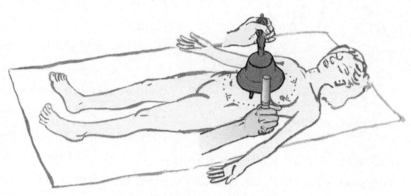

Sing ganta above heart clockwise.

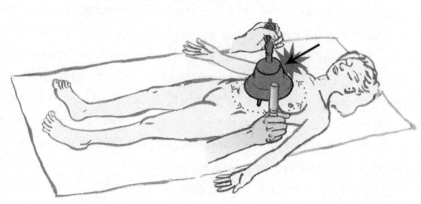

Strike then sing ganta counter clockwise above heart.

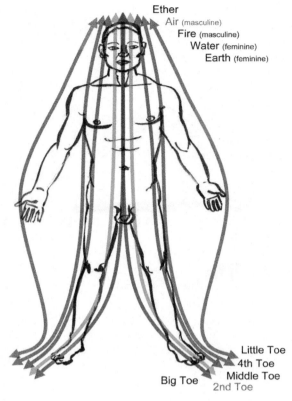

Ether
Air (masculine)
Fire (masculine)
Water (feminine)
Earth (feminine)

Little Toe
4th Toe
Middle Toe
Big Toe   2nd Toe

Elemental long lines.

Note: It is important to clear the long lines of the body with the ganta and the emotional body with the crystal dorje at the feet before doing any bowl work. (See Resources for workshops that cover long lines and emotional bodywork.)

Bowl Work

The bowl work you do for depression is the opposite of what you would do for anxiety. Anxiety is very much the fire element and you want to bring that energy down. But with depression, you want to create deep relaxation and strengthen the ability to find joy. Remember that someone who is depressed needs to take very tiny baby steps toward joy. They cannot be asked to take any large steps because their sense of hopelessness makes it likely they will turn back toward themselves. Sound healing in this case is really about helping someone find a sense of joy in very small things and building on that.

To this end it would be effective to establish some nurturing activities they can do between sessions, and have them check in with you about these from time to time. You can invite them to call or email you to report on how they are doing with their homework. To assign this homework, you might ask, for example, "What might you do that is nurturing for yourself?" Once they establish two or three nurturing things that they feel will affect them positively, you can set up a check-in program for accountability.

The accountability factor is especially important with depression because it's easy for someone who is depressed to just not do the work—

typically, by definition, they lack motivation. So make sure your checking-in system doesn't take a lot of effort. You can say, "Pop me an email and let me know how you're doing between now and the next session. Doing that will help shift your energy." That way they are responsible outside the session for doing some of the work that will help in their healing.

Another important aspect is to lighten up—literally. The way you touch the person and play the instruments should have a light, etheric quality to help "call out" the person from their inward-focused state. You want to work with gentle fire and etheric energy, not dynamite.

Everything you do will be soothing and light: a lot of singing the bowls and building the pace from slow to quick, with a light touch when striking the bowls. This is one of the cases where, after an initial grounding and clearing of stuck energy, you can work the triads with the apex going upward. Working up from the feet, you might begin with:

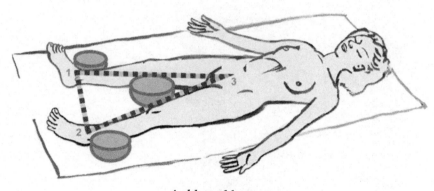

Ankle-ankle-root.

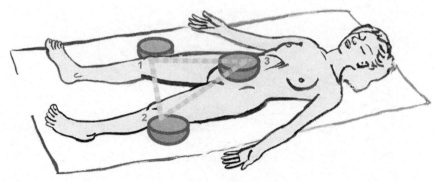

Knee-knee-sacrum.

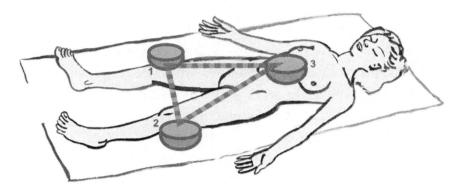

Knee-knee-solar plexus.

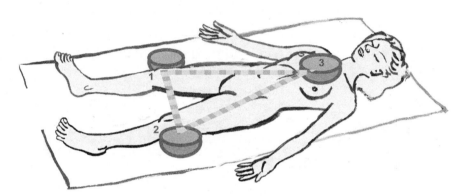

Knee-knee-heart.

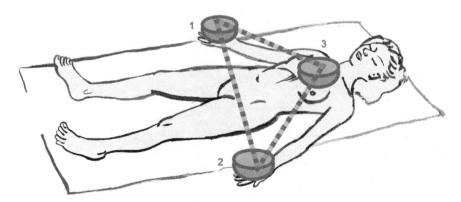

Hand-hand-heart.

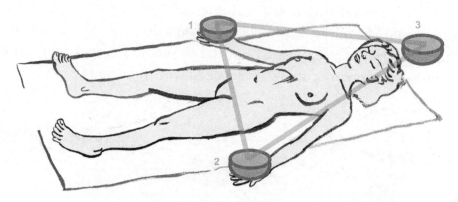

Hand-hand-crown.

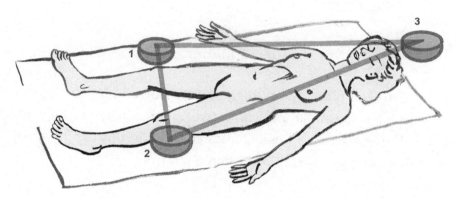

Knee-knee-crown.

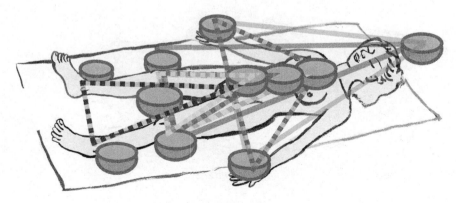

Ankle to crown triads.

Make those stabilizing triads with the energy going upward, and work with the chakras from foot through root, sacrum, solar, heart, and all the way up. It is best to use a crystal on the throat and crown rather than a bowl, and then work just above these areas with your bowls.

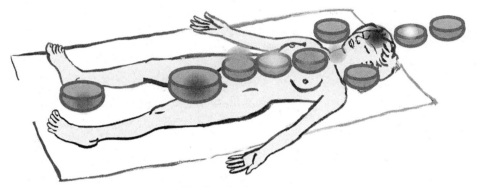

Up the chakras.

You might even place a very high-pitched bowl above the crown bowl to create a lovely rhythmic and sonic river. Remember, too, that you can always lift the energy of a person from their body upward by creating a triad and then using a bowl to lift it into a pyramid.

Lifting energy.

This really brings the energy up, and someone who's depressed needs that.

You can work with the fire and ether lines as well. To find the ether line, touch the center of your collarbone and feel the two bumps on either side. In between the bumps there's a fleshy triangle: if you push in there, you'll start gagging—you're on the ether line, which is really your central core. The fire line is about halfway between the central core and the outside edge of your body, all the way down the front of your body on either side of the central ether line. (It runs right over the nipple.)

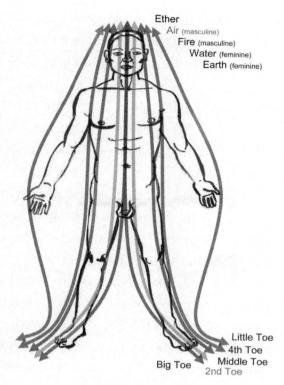

Elemental long lines.

After a few sessions, it would be appropriate to do some advanced work on your partner's back with the governing and conceptual vessel meridians. This will help bring to consciousness aspects that are unconscious but will greatly impact them positively. (See Resources for a DVD that covers this.)

The tingshas awaken energy, so with someone who's suffering from depression, feel free to work with tingshas a little bit more than usual. Sometimes you will see that one area is still very stuck, even though you have tried many ways to move the energy. You can then go back to gently waking up the energy there with the tingshas—and with compassion because fragility and fear are present there.

Do not rush through using relaxing touch to help the client feel nurtured and safe—take your time. People tend to feel guilty about being depressed, so whatever you say needs to convey that it is safe for them to feel whatever they feel. Underneath the depression there are usually other feelings that want and need expression.

Toning is great for depression. The aim is to create a sustained and soothing sound they can release into. Invite them to tone an open-mouthed "ahhh," extending the exhalation. "Ah" is the Sanskrit sound of the heart opening, so the tone creates a feeling of loving energy they can release and surrender their feelings into. You might sing a bowl and "ah" with them for a little while to help get them started. Sometimes people are shy about making sounds, and you need to find creative ways to help them relax into the "ah."

If there's a lot of grief, you might invite them to tone the sound of the grief in order to get it out of their body. Sometimes people just don't have a clue about how to do that, so give them some textural places to start by asking them whether their grief would sound like a metallic, high-pitched tone or a soft, squishy tone. Ask, "Is the sound a very low, thudding sound, or is it like a scraping, or is it a cry? Does it have a vowel sound, or does it sound like wood or water?" Then support whatever little sound ekes out of them, encouraging them to get louder and let the sound become fuller, to get the sound out of their body. Again, it may help if you make the sound with them.

If you have a gong, this is a good time to use it too, for a couple of reasons. It's kind of like singing along with the radio; hearing another, different sound tends to help people express themselves. Also, they'll be less self-conscious, and as you get louder with the gong, you can encourage them to get louder too.

Depression is a volatile *and* a heavy energy. I've seen clients come out of their depression during the treatment and feel really great. Then after they leave, one, tiny little thing happens and they catapult right back into it. This is why it is helpful to get the emotions out of the body—it helps create resilience. And this is why giving homework for them to do between sessions is also an important part of increasing the impact of the session work—they need that structure to fall back on.

One of my students made a comment that leads to an important point:

I haven't worked much with people in depression, so this is really fasci-nating. What really resonates with me is the whole light aspect of it …

keeping it light, bringing light in. They're feeling so heavy, and there is a part of me that feels there is a way to use the bowls, the gantas, the tingshas so that they almost sound playful at times.

This is true, and it's why it's so important for you to gain mastery at creating the many nuances of your sound tools by changing how you touch and play them to create soothing, energizing, awakening—and yes, playful—sounds.

A Depression Case Study

A very depressed female client had energy like dense clay. It had no air at all, and all the life seemed to have gone out of her. Her energy was so heavy, like tar, that I had to work very hard myself to stay grounded and not be pulled down into it. She had just moved to the area and hated her job and where she was living. She kept making a lot of comparisons to where she had been before, yet she had moved because she hadn't been happy where she was before either. In conversations with her, she said a lot of "but" this and "but" that. It's important in a situation like this to just witness and create a space for the person to share whatever they feel.

I could see that she was arguing for her limitations and not partnering with me or accepting responsibility for her healing. At one point when I felt her energy wasn't moving at all, I asked her if she felt relaxed and if she felt energy moving. "Oh yeah," she said, "I'm always relaxed during these sessions." And then she said, "Well, my shoulders and neck are really tight and the muscles are contracted, but that's normal." I suggested that if she were truly relaxed, the muscles probably wouldn't be tight. She countered with a lot of reasons why she could be relaxed with tense muscles.

In this case, the woman was truly working against me, although she wasn't doing it consciously. I recognized that at least she was getting herself to the sessions. But when she was with me, she was holding tight to herself and arguing for her limitations in words as well as on cellular, physical, and energetic levels.

She was stuck in her story and so afraid to let go. I had to keep holding the space open for her and being with her at her own pace. This was a situation in which it was hard for my ego not to get involved. I wanted to push her to go faster than she was going, and I was working hard just to stay present and not get sucked in while being a willing witness for her to work at her own pace.

I did a lot of work on the fire meridians going up her body, as well as advanced governing and conceptual vessel work, which brings the unconscious into the conscious.

After the final session to address her depression she emailed me to tell me that she had found a new job. So something did shift—she got out of the job she hated and found herself a new one. She then wanted another fire session to help motivate and root her in confidence about the new things in her life.

The long and the short of it is that whatever was going on, I was able to hold the space for her without my ego getting involved and without pushing for her to do anything. I just mirrored and encouraged her, and the shift did eventually happen. So while the work was challenging, it had a positive outcome.

The following story comes from one of my students, who works with a lot of instruments and sound in her own practice.

> I integrate other sound stuff because I'm a classically trained musician and have many instruments and have done other work with sound for many, many years. And I have some African hardwood drums that are just incredibly happy drums. They have a sound that can't help but make you smile when you hear it. Even though I said I haven't worked much with depression, I have worked with a few people who are depressed, and I've worked quite a bit with people who are grieving.
>
> The African hardwood drums have this amazing uplifting effect. After working with the bowls, maybe I'll even use some other instruments to let them be in the grief for a period of time. But I'll end the session with the African hardwood drums

because their happy sound brings them up. The sound of those drums lifts them up and brings light, and it's just a really wonderful thing.

I agree with that, and in my own practice I also use rattles because they feel like they're going into every little nook and cranny and grabbing any little particle that's hiding out. I'll shake those particles up to be cleared out and aligned with the bowls.

The important thing is to know why you are doing what you're doing, not to just arbitrarily grab one instrument or another. For someone who's depressed, if you decide to work with a drum or with gongs, I recommend you work from the feet up. And be careful not to blast them, because they're very vulnerable. Gongs are also very good for clearing out stuck energy.

You now have plenty of information on using the Himalayan instruments to shift and balance energy. If you did nothing but practice all the techniques you have learned so far, that would be a lot! In my practice, though, I also use other healing modalities to augment the sacred sound work. These are the subject of Part V.

Part V

Enhancing Your Practice

Are you ready to add a few more items to your sound healing repertoire? I find that colors and toning, visualization, and introducing clients to power language are all powerful tools for healing that integrate wonderfully with the work with the instruments.

Chapter 17

COLORS AND TONING

There are excellent books and workshops available on both of the topics covered in this short chapter on using color and toning for healing. My aim here is to get you thinking about the possibilities—which are many—and to let you know that you can use both to enhance your sessions. I highly recommend that advanced practitioners and students take the time to develop expertise in both areas. These are also areas you will learn more about in my own advanced workshop series (see Further Resources).

Using Color

We know that color is a higher vibration of sound, and that many people see colors during a sound healing treatment. We also know that each color has a unique set of attributes that can help restore balance on all levels. When you use color in conjunction with sound, you can help nourish and balance exhausted or blocked parts of your clients' physical, emotional, or spiritual selves and create powerful transformation.

There are many ways to use color during a session. I will mention a few things I do, and then you can let your imagination run and see what methods you might like to try.

Sometimes I use color cards with the symbolism of each color written on the back. I ask clients to choose two cards; the first one picked represents where they are now (emotionally and energetically) and the second represents an aspect of themselves they are strengthening. At the end of the session, I read the meanings—they are usually spot-on.

Another way I use color is to invite the client to visualize a certain color and breathe it into their body or a part of their body to bring relief or to strengthen. I also have a variety of colored scarves; I select one that corresponds to the client's issue and place it on them during a session.

Toning

Toning—making sounds with the voice—is a powerful way to work with sound that clients can easily do on their own. You may recall that I touched on this a little when I suggested that the sound "aaahh" toned at the beginning of a session could help your clients relax into the moment. That was just a taste of how you might make use of toning.

No matter where we go, our voice and our breath are with us. Sounds or tones emerge from us naturally to express feelings, release pain, provide relief, and restore the natural flow of energy to the body, creating a therapeutic and restorative effect on the body/mind. Recall that the human body is made up largely of water, which is a highly successful transmitter of energy. This is why toning followed by playing the Tibetan bowls directly on the body has a profound effect on the nervous system and the entire body.

The practice of toning can be as simple as identifying the sounds we make naturally to express emotions and repeating them with clear intention for several minutes each. Think *ah, oh*—vowel sounds are quite effective. You can also tone mantras or syllables that contain specific vibrations. These clear the chakras and calm the mind when repeated for several minutes several times a day. The most familiar example and one of the most powerful is *Aum* or *Om,* the mantra of universal perfection.

Basic Toning

To tone as part of your sound healing practice, sit or stand with your spine straight but relaxed. Then exhale a long, sustained sound for the duration of your breath. It's that simple.

Toning, Trust, and the Inner Critic

I initiate a toning practice only for clients with whom I have established a strong sense of trust. That's because expressing sound in the presence of another person can strongly trigger the voice of the inner critic, a voice that must be quieted in order for the client to produce their own "right sound." Then sympathetic resonance can be achieved between voice and bowl and transmitted through the body, and great energetic releases can result.

Toning for Yourself

You can clear your own chakras using tone, and you can find your own tone and use it to release stuck energy and center yourself, or to generate peace and compassion. Being able to find and express your personal tone—the one that, when uttered, opens your heart and sends energy through your entire body—gives you a powerful tool to shift out of energetic blocks and illness by entraining with higher-level frequencies. Further, if you can match your tone with a Himalayan bowl of the same frequency and play it directly on your body, you can release negative patterns and open yourself to expanded consciousness and a higher level of energy.

Exercise: Toning to Clear the Chakras

In his book *Healing Sounds*, Jonathan Goldman offers a simple toning exercise that is great for clearing chakras and is very energizing.[5] Tone each of the following sounds seven times. Note that each tone, working from the root to the crown, gets progressively higher in pitch.

> **First Chakra (Root—Red):** Tone with the deepest *uuh*, as in "cup," a very low, guttural sound gently riding on the breath.

Second Chakra (Sacral—Orange): Use higher-pitched but still deep *ooo*, as in "you."

Third Chakra (Solar Plexus—Yellow): Use a higher-pitched *oh*, as in "go."

Fourth Chakra (Heart—Green): Use a higher-pitched *ah*, as in "Ma." This is the sound that embodies compassion.

Fifth Chakra (Throat—Blue): Use a higher-pitched *eye*, as in "my."

Sixth Chakra (Third Eye—Indigo): Use a still higher-pitched *ay*, as in "say."

Seventh Chakra (Crown—Violet or White): Use the highest-pitched *eee* sound, as in "me," that you can comfortably make.

Now sit in a space of silence and receptivity for ten to twenty minutes to experience the energy of your toning. If you feel light-headed, you can tone *aaaah* to bring energy back to the heart and then an *ooooh* to bring energy down to the sacral area to become more grounded.

Chapter 18
Visualization

Visualization is an excellent way to work directly with the subconscious to access the parts of ourselves that need acknowledgment, strengthening, and/or releasing. The sacred sound instruments themselves access cognitive, cellular, emotional, and spiritual aspects within each person. Adding visualization helps support the work you do with the instruments, creating more powerful shifts. It also helps clients feel more ownership of their healing sessions, since it calls for participation.

Any effective visualization will guide the client into *his or her* inner journey and expression. This means that practitioners should refrain from projecting their own agenda onto the client, though this happens all too often. Guided meditation leaders sometimes describe every little detail of where they want clients to go in the session, but I think this is a mistake. Visualization isn't about our vision of what we want for our clients; rather, our job is to set up a context in which our clients can discover intimate parts of themselves—for themselves.

A good visualization uses very few words and just enough structure to help the client access their inner world. It is important to practice guiding visualizations aloud so you can deliver them seamlessly at a low volume and a gentle, slow pace. In this chapter I'll give you the practice tools you need to do this. By memorizing the scripts that appear here, taping them, and playing them back to yourself during your own meditation, you will get an idea of what works and what doesn't.

Create a Repertoire in Advance

It is a good idea to create a repertoire of possible guided visualizations with practice partners. As you conduct your practice sessions, you will find patterns emerging in terms of what people want and what they come to you for. These themes may include the desire for more creativity, joy, self-confidence, abundance, and empowerment. If you create visualizations tailored to these themes, you can use them over and over again.

Choose textural language that invites people to travel into *their* hearts and consciousness, rather than into yours. The idea is for them to explore their own inner world. And don't be afraid to drop the affirmation and make use of silence, as quiet stretches give people the time to manifest their vision—this is actually where they will do most of their work. Silence is the place they can expand into when you are conducting a sound healing session. It is also the place you expand into during your meditations.

Using Bowls with Visualization

During a guided visualization, it is helpful to use the bowls as an anchor. The idea here is to create a neutral rhythm and volume: a background drone. As you get to know your instruments you will learn to elicit lots of different nuances from them. Some of these are very soothing and some are energizing. A neutral rhythm emerges when you play a *very slow, very soft, consistent pattern* with just a few bowls while you speak. You may use just one for a specific chakra if you are focusing on that, or you can use the head triad. And you can either strike or sing.

How to Keep the Focus on the Client

Shortly I'll cover several good guided visualizations for the inner masculine, inner feminine, and inner healer. You can create your own versions; however, be very careful about your wording. Here is an example of what *not* to say for the inner feminine visualization.

> "Okay, I'm inviting you to bring into your consciousness your perception of your divine inner female. She's a white light, she's really beautiful, and she has wings."

This language leads the client into *your* vision of the divine inner female. To avoid this, simply invite them to bring their own inner female into their perception by saying something like this:

> "She might appear to you as a form or an element or color. Tune in to how she appears to you. These are her attributes: wisdom, unconditional love, creativity, and the ability to nurture."

Although here you offer a few attributes, notice that you haven't described anything else—you have left it to the client to visualize how those qualities might take form. What they see in their mind's eye is entirely their own creation.

You might give your client this kind of direction a couple of times, repeating the attributes. Then say:

> "When you have a sense of your divine inner female, move your lips or move a finger of your right hand."

Here you have given them a way to communicate without having to say anything. Then just wait for them. That's the beginning. Then you might say:

"Okay, we want to strengthen her within you. We want to strengthen her frequency. We want to strengthen her attributes, raise her. When you've done that, move your fingers."

You can see that the client is doing most of the work. They aren't being led by the hand with something like "She has beautiful robes and flowing hair and she's walking down a path toward a lake, and the lake is crystal clear, and she enters the purity of the lake and goes to the bottom and finds a diamond …"

Words: Less Is More

Whether it's a group or a private session, when it comes to words, less is more. Many people are uncomfortable with silence so they jump in to fill it with words. When you're doing a visualization and working with someone's subconscious, times of silence are where fear starts coming up. It's also where inner nudgings and inklings happen, and we have a chance to hear the messages we normally dismiss or interfere with through noise and distractions.

When we meditate silently, does that mean there's nothing going on? No! There's a lot going on. We are creating a container for what I would call ethereal and intuitive voices so they can emerge and be heard within the silence. If you have experienced guided visualizations where the speaker never stops talking, you know that there isn't a lot of room for your inner voice. Fortunately, you can take a different, more effective approach.

Common Issues for Visualization Work

Issues that lend themselves to guided visualization include:

- Pain
- Lack of power
- Self-confidence
- Procrastination
- Creativity

- Ungroundedness
- Health
- Heart opening
- Self-honor
- Vitality
- Inspiration
- Motivation
- Connection
- Relationship

I have developed visualizations to address all of these issues because they keep coming up for people. I recommend that as you develop your practice, you do the same.

Working with the Auric Field: Exercise

Now let's start practicing visualization. This first technique is effective at the end of a session to help strengthen self-confidence and presence and to help people learn to feel their energy field. It also expands the clearing/ healing work that has been done during the session. *Note:* do not do this activity if anxiety or depression is present.

The subtle energy field around the body, also known as the auric field, is not a mystery. It is simply a part of ourselves—a vital one—that many people have a limited awareness of and relationship with. This energy field helps us to align with spirit and our environment.

Have you ever been at a party or another kind of gathering and felt small tinges of shyness or embarrassment? Or maybe the opposite: you're in a small space feeling like you're going to explode. These are some of the signs that you are out of alignment with your auric field. Your energy system is operating of its own accord and you're just along for the ride. In the latter case you need to draw in your energetic field. If you want to be more social at a party, raise your vibration and expand your energy field before you enter the room. This can help you to interact with people and draw them to you.

The following exercise is a way to get familiar with your subtle energy system and expand your potential for protection, healing, and power. You can do this exercise for yourself in everyday life and with your clients as a way to stay centered and aligned, as well as to gauge the amount of presence you want to have in a particular situation. There are situations where you may want to be invisible and others where you really want to be seen. You can draw your field in tightly if you are in a situation where you want to just observe, or if you are walking somewhere alone and don't want to attract attention. Do you want your boss to see your value more before you approach her for a raise? Or do you have an audition, or a meeting to run? These would be great times to raise and expand your energy field.

Important note: As you work your way through the following script, speak slowly and softly. Pause between sentences so your client or practice partner has time to visualize what you are saying. Speak the first sentence twice, slowly, to help the person bring their consciousness to the task at hand, as they may be in an altered state of awareness. Memorizing scripts is the best way to deliver them and sound natural.

Script

Please imagine a shaft of white light coming in through the top of your head [pause, then repeat]. Please imagine a shaft of white light coming in through the top of your head. [pause] and moving all the way down the core of your body [pause], through the root chakra and into the ground [pause]. Now begin to strengthen that shaft of light until it explodes in rays in all directions [pause]. As the shaft becomes stronger, it expands within you and begins to shoot out rays of light in all directions [pause]. Keep expanding your energetic blueprint out through your body [pause] through the walls of the room [pause], into the street [pause]. Now begin to draw the energy back in from the street [pause], into the room [pause], and into your body [pause]. Feel it vibrating there throughout your core [pause]. Strengthen the vibration in your core [pause]. This time you will expand the energetic field to where you are comfortable [pause]. How far outside your body do you want your auric field to go? [Pause.] Place it there [pause].

French Press Breathing Exercise

This breathing exercise is particularly good to practice to move pain out of the body. You can also use it to move out emotions such as anger, fear, or grief. And you might choose to do this exercise at the beginning of a session to draw attention away from distress.

Ask the person to imagine that their body is a French press coffee maker. Have them visualize placing their hands on the top of their head, where they will work the piston of the French press. Ask them to inhale with short breaths and then exhale with full, slow breaths as they see their hands pushing downward, moving pain or emotions through the body from head to foot and out the bottoms of the feet. If there is a particular place in the body where they get stuck, tell them they can imagine many more hands coming in to push the sensation or emotion down and out of the body.

You may sing a bowl or a ganta while walking the client through this exercise.

Divine Feminine Exercise

The purpose of this exercise is to awaken aspects of the Divine Feminine within your client or practice partner. Practice this exercise about three-quarters into a session so it leaves a strong imprint for the person to take home with them.

Script

I invite you to awaken the Divine Feminine within you. She may come in many different forms: perhaps an entity, a color, an element, or a sensation. Invite your perception of your inner Divine Feminine into your consciousness. When you have done so, please indicate this by moving your finger.

Her attributes are unconditional love, great wisdom, and the cycles of creativity. Transmute the energy—the vibrational frequency of your Divine Inner Feminine—to an even higher vibration. When you have done so, please indicate by moving your finger.

Now transmute your Divine Feminine to the apex of her potential, to the highest frequency of her potential. You are the gatekeeper for the energy of the Divine Feminine. You are the one who knows how to nourish her so she will stay strong within you. Tell me—in a whisper—what she needs from you to keep her vibrant and strong within.

Let's say the person you are working with responds by saying, "faith and patience."

Give her your faith. She needs patience. You have patience! Extend your patience to her.

Then ask the person if the Divine Feminine needs anything else. If not, say *"She is complete."*

You can do the same exercise for the Divine Masculine and the Divine Inner Healer, replacing the characteristics of each as follows:

- The qualities of Divine Masculine include strength (physical, mental, spiritual, and emotional), compassion, and the ability to manifest in the physical world.
- The qualities of Divine Inner Healer include unconditional love, self-honor, discernment, and the ability to act on your own behalf, standing up for yourself.

Heart Opening

This is good to do after your tingshas diagnosis and your opening moves, when your client or practice partner has started to become relaxed.

Script

Please bring into your consciousness the image of a beautiful high mountain lake [pause]. The water is crystal clear and so pure you can see your image in it [pause]. You stand at the edge looking in. The water is so still you can see the little grasses moving at the bottom [pause]. A stone is thrown in, causing expanding circles [pause]. Each circle touches the next and the next, expanding out farther and farther, like the circles of your heart [pause]. The circles keep growing larger with you in the center, in love's embrace [pause]. From the outer edges of the ever-expanding circle, you can see yourself through the eyes of love [pause]. What you see is all your gifts, all your accomplishments, your celebrations and triumphs [pause]. You also see all your perceived failures, your challenges, your idiosyncrasies [pause]. You see the totality of your life combined to create the unique and divine being that you are. Take a moment to breathe into this and open your heart to your whole self.

After a final pause, continue with your session.

Identifying a Sound Exercise

You can use this technique when your client or practice partner is having difficulty resolving a feeling of being stuck. It is most effective either toward the beginning of a session or in the middle. *Note:* Be sure you have established trust between yourself and the person before doing this exercise.

Have the client select an issue they have been dealing with. Then direct them to produce sounds until they find one that is a good reflection of the issue they want to resolve. It could be any sound: rattling, gurgling, screeching, or something else. When they seem to have settled on one, ask, "Does this sound really represent the issue?" They may decide that it doesn't quite express the issue after all. Coach the person to explore a variety of sounds until they find the sound that truly fits.

Next, ask, "Where is it in your body?" Invite them to allow the sound to increase in volume, to let it get bigger, to let it overtake the body. Leave room for the sound to evolve into a different sound ... and then encourage the client to just breathe for a while.

Next, have the person imagine the most beautiful sound and encourage them to make that sound. Ask them to extend the length of the beautiful sound, allowing it to become more melodic, like a muse, and allowing it to expand into their entire body—arms, legs, capillaries, bloodstream.

Remind the person that the next time they encounter this issue or are in a similar situation, they can make this sound, making it aloud if they are in a safe place to do so, or internally if that would not be appropriate. Tell them they can use this tool at any time.

Breathing Down

This breathing technique is effective at the very start of a session while the client is seated.

- After minimal chitchat when they first arrive, invite your client or practice partner to close their eyes and relax. This will be grounding and centering for both of you. Ask them to notice if they are holding energy or tension anywhere.
- Invite them to release any held energy or tension.
- Invite them to drop the breath into the sacrum. (Observe to see if you notice the breath doing this—you may see a general relaxing of the shoulders or a sigh.)
- Invite them to slow their heartbeat and respiration.

Deep Listening

Doing the Breathing Down technique helps bring your client or practice partner into the present moment. Take it slowly with this, allowing time for the person to really tune in to each different aspect. As they relax into the moment, you may see their facial expression soften or they may sigh. If there is a lot of fluttering in the eyes or fidgeting, this is a clue that they are still in their head and are have trouble relaxing. Once it looks like they have achieved some measure of relaxation, ask them to:

- Tune in to the sound of the breath entering and leaving the body
- See if they can feel and hear their heartbeat
- Extend their focus to hearing the sounds inside the room
- Extend their focus to hearing the sounds outside the room
- Bring their focus back into the room
- Bring their focus back into the body, to their heartbeat and breath

Now allow them to be silent in their observations for a while.

Wholeness

You can do this exercise after the initial relaxation on the mat. This is a good sequence to follow when the intention is "I am connected to my wholeness."

With your hands on the persons' ankles, say in a slow, quiet voice, "Wholeness is not your work, your activities, your relationships, your tasks, or your body. Wholeness is the divine light energy that you came into this lifetime with and that will remain infinitely, long after you have left your body.

"In a moment you will be invited to quietly, in a whisper, say a few sentences. As you say each statement, notice even the slightest shift in your energy as it begins to slowly move and release. Let's begin:

- *Move your hands up to the knees.* Say: "Please whisper, 'Who I am.'"
- *Move your hands to just above the root/ sacrum area.* Then say: "As you say this, *Who I am not* lines up and makes an exit out the top

of your head, releasing ineffective belief systems that no longer serve you."

- *Move your hands to the heart.* Say: "Your wholeness is the ability to love yourself unconditionally and to honor all parts of yourself. Please say, *'Who I am in relationship to my heart.'"* (The ability to love oneself unconditionally with great compassion is a path to healing—and you can say this too.)
- *Move your hands to the throat* (do not touch). Say: "Sabotaging wholeness is self-judgment, shame, words of blame, and criticism I carry with me from others or myself. These are ways we turn against ourselves. Please say, *'How I have turned against myself.'"*
- *Move your hands to the crown.* Say: "Wholeness is the balance between giving and receiving. Please say, *'Who I am in perfect balance between giving and receiving.'"*

I think you will find that visualization can really help your practice partners and clients open to unexpected insights and experience their diamond selves. I hope you enjoy it!

Chapter 19

POWER LANGUAGE

In my prior work as a life coach, I saw the powerful shifts that took place when I helped my clients change their language habits. I have since incorporated working with language in my sound healing practice and have seen it create real and positive differences in people's lives. Now I would like to share some of these language techniques with you. I will frame most of this discussion in terms of how you can help your practice partners and then clients, but these lessons in language apply to you as well—this is an opportunity to sensitize yourself to your own language habits.

Sound healing is a lot of things. Yes, it's Tibetan bowls, gantas, and tingshas. It's also working with self-talk and how our clients express themselves to others. Sound healing includes the ability to recognize patterns that our practice partners and clients reveal through their choice of words.

Words reflect belief systems. When we incorporate power language into sound healing, it's our job to gently mirror back to people the words they're using that keep them stuck. For example, clients say things like "Well, I'm not good at this," or "I always procrastinate," or "I am so disorganized." My response? *"You don't have to attach yourself to that belief."*

As I pointed out very early in the book when discussing frameworks for healing, people say self-limiting things all the time without even being aware of it. We tend to judge ourselves by what we perceive as our personality's "weakest link." You'll find that when people come in for sessions with you, they'll say derogatory things about themselves or say other things that key you into a belief system they have or a judgment they hold about themselves.

The Power of "I Choose"

"I choose" is a great example of power language. It's often the case that people don't communicate what they want or need very well, either to themselves or others. Examples of this are the often-used phrases *I need to, I want to, I have to, I should,* and *I'll try to.* These words set people up with behavioral loopholes—that is, these are words that are noncommittal and help them avoid really taking responsibility. Just feel the shift in energy when replacing any of these phrases above with *I choose to.* Suddenly you have brought in a feeling of immediacy and a sense of accountability.

Becoming a Mirror

Where language is concerned, our job is to very gently mirror clients' belief systems, limiting self-talk, and behaviors so they don't have to keep pigeonholing themselves with self-depreciating inner chatter, ineffective beliefs, and poor communication. The work with the sacred sound instruments helps raise awareness of these things and then strengthens aspects of the self that help shift patterns from ineffective to effective, strong, and positive. A client might say to me, "I need to get grounded because I never follow through on things and I want to get organized."

"Well, do you have a family?" I ask.
"Yes."
"Did you shop for the family this week?"
"Yeah."
"Did you take your kids to school?"
"Yeah."

"Did you do any laundry?"

"Yeah."

"Did you make dinner for your family?"

"Yeah."

"Did you make their lunches?"

"Yeah."

"Well, it looks like you're pretty organized in a lot of ways," I say. "What area are you judging yourself on?"

"Oh, it's my office."

"Oh, so you've got clutter in your office, and because you have clutter in your office, you see the whole of yourself as a messy, disorganized person."

This kind of mirroring can be very eye opening for your clients. When you encounter language like this, you can help them shift that perspective and assume a larger and more positive vision of themselves. This gives them a stronger foundation to build upon than just this one weak area. An astute sound healing practitioner is aware of people's choice of words and can remind clients that they don't have to attach themselves to their negative judgments and limiting word choices.

Assertive Versus Aggressive

Something else to keep in mind is that people often lack the confidence to speak up for themselves, at home or on the job. They see themselves as smaller than they really are because they don't yet understand the difference between being assertive and being aggressive. They believe they will come across as aggressive if they express their needs. This is especially true for women.

Being assertive is nothing more than clearly expressing your needs. Many women have a tendency to do something like the following (I call it "taking the temperature"):

A woman says to her husband, "Honey, do you want to go to a movie tonight?"

Honey is in the middle of doing something and replies, "No, thanks."

Honey's wife says to herself, *He never wants to do anything with me.*

That's a typical way of communicating without saying what you really want. What this woman really meant was "I want to go to the movies tonight and I'd love it if you came with me." This more direct way of communicating forces you to get into the habit of being vulnerable because you're reporting what your real feelings are. So start to pay attention and to get to know what your own feelings are. It's great practice for introducing power language into your sound healing work.

Years ago, I was walking on the beach with Richard, and I said, "Richard, why don't you take your shoes off so you can walk barefoot in the sand?"

He said, "No. I'm perfectly comfortable with my shoes on."

"Yeah, but the sand is really great and it's good for you to walk barefoot," I said.

"Yeah, but you know I'll walk barefoot when I feel like it. Right now I'm fine."

I thought about it for a little while and then finally said, "You know, walking barefoot in the beach is something really special for me and I'd like to share it with you."

And he threw off his shoes and said, "Well, why didn't you say that in the first place?"

The lesson in this example is that people want to please each other. But some people need more direct instruction on how to do that. In general, people are very happy to know that they can do something for you—if they know it's for *you.*

A Definition of Power Language

How would I define power language? It's the combination of the right words spoken at the right time and in the right way to enable us to get more of what we want, more of the time. There are two recipients of words: self and other. And the good news about the words we say to ourselves is that we can cultivate the ability to change our own self-talk from negative to positive, silencing that internal chatter we have running in our minds all the time: the self-critic, the judge, the naysayer, the insidious saboteur. This is the voice of the backseat driver of our life, and it is so ingrained in the texture of who we are that we really have to exert special attention to hear, recognize, and shift that dynamic.

When it comes to the words we use with others, there's a structure to being assertive rather than aggressive. It's a very specific pattern that people can learn, and it's best to try it out with mundane, everyday situations so that when a situation is charged you can access it easily.

Elements of Powerful Communication

Self-Talk

The quality of your self-talk greatly affects your reality and thus how you communicate.

As I said before, self-talk is a backseat driver with the power to steer your life, whether you're aware of it or not. It can either be powerfully constructive or it can covertly usurp your every effort. A simple way to test this for yourself is to go to a strenuous exercise class where they're kicking your butt, having you do demanding things like pushups and sit-ups. Notice the difference in your energy pattern when you absentmindedly say to yourself, *"Oh, God, I can't do this. Not one more, I'm so tired."* Then interrupt that pattern and change it to *"I love doing sit-ups. I know I can do at least five more!"* You can literally feel the energy shift when you start encouraging yourself rather than berating yourself.

It might be of interest to look at what creates internal chatter or self-talk in the first place.

Studies have shown that what we think, feel, like, dislike, and believe originate from the unconscious patterns we formed as children. In fact, the personality traits we formed as young as preschool age remain with us as adults.[6] And since our basic personalities were formed early, the messages we got during that time from our families, our cultures, and our environment impacted us a lot. I don't only mean "You're a bad boy/girl" messages. I also mean "Don't do that" or "Be careful" or "No, sweetie." These messages block the natural instinct of a child to explore.

Many of these messages are for the child's own safety, of course, but think about a child's natural curiosity and how when a hand grabs her and holds her back, or she hears a sharp-voiced "No," the experience is a negative, not a positive one. It is important to look for ways, especially when it comes to safety, to encourage our children, while at the same time letting them know when something is dangerous—being clear that we're not criticizing them, because that's how they tend to experience it.

Add to this the fact that we have about 60,000 thoughts per day, 90 percent of which are repeated day after day.[7] Think about that—90 percent of the things you say to yourself today are things you're going to repeat tomorrow and the day after tomorrow and the day after that, and you don't even realize you're doing it. Now you have a picture of where your chatter comes from and how it works. A lot of it comes from your unconscious, and although you don't know it's there, it sabotages your efforts. That also means you have about 10 percent of space left for new, ingenious "aha" moments—unless you clear out the ineffective patterns.

Mirroring the Positive

You might be saying to yourself, "Okay, but how does this information apply to sound healing?" My job as a practitioner is to see and mirror back everything that is positive in my client. I need to see their perfection because I know I may be the only one who lets them know that they're beautiful and unique, and that all of the crap they have in their life is really wonderful compost for the beautiful life they're growing into. It's not trash—it's fertilizer because it has given them depth, and their hard experiences help them be compassionate to others who have a hard time. It is the practitioner's job to help clients gain a different and larger perspective:

the gift within the wound. I can only do that if I see their perfection, reflect it back to them, and choose words that help them to see it too.

So how do we change internal chatter? Practice. You're not going to change your body if you only go to the gym once. One yoga class isn't going to do you a whole lot of good. Everything we learn, we learn through repetition; it's how we learn to talk and speak and read. So we take that understanding and bring it to the behavioral patterns we choose to change.

In the same way, we shift the behavioral patterns of our practice partners and clients. We develop awareness, create positive affirmations, and give ourselves enough cues to remember to practice in a more effective way. During your sessions, through the awareness and positive affirmations you create during client intake, you can help your clients find the right words to express what their real needs are. Most of the time when you hit on something that's a core issue, people will start tearing up or have another kind of physical reaction. When that happens, you know you're just hit the nail on the head. Now you know what they *really* came in to work on.

Choosing the Right Words

What are the right words to use with power language? They're words that clearly represent your truth but contain no shaming, blaming, guilt-tripping, or criticism of yourself or another person. My personal platform in my life, which I'm constantly being given the opportunity to live up to, comes from Angeles Arrien's *The Four-Fold Way* (my own wording in parentheses follows Angeles's):[8]

- Show up. (Bring yourself to the situation in the present moment.)
- Pay attention. (Bring your awareness to present moment.)
- Speak your truth without shaming or blaming. (Use "I" statements.)
- Let go of the outcome. (Like a good affirmation, take an action because it is the best, most effective, right thing to do. Acting so you will get your way becomes manipulation.)

The Right Timing

The next thing to consider is timing, and again, let's start with your own timing. Start practicing this with your family because this is really important—timing is sticky but it can be learned. It requires listening and observing body language that indicates openness, interest, or fatigue.

We all have been in a conversation with someone and desperately want the conversation to end, but the other person doesn't get it. You're looking at your watch, you're backing up, but the person isn't reading any of your "I want this to end" cues. Sound familiar? And have you been in a situation where you've gotten those cues from someone else and you've persisted to drive your point home, whether they want to hear it or not?

The best time to bring up something important with your spouse probably isn't the moment they walk in the door after work. We all do it though, don't we?—we're just champing at the bit to share whatever that important thing is. That is called *bad timing*.

But you can create the appropriate time to be heard. In a meeting you might say, "I'd like your attention so I can share something important" and then wait until you get that attention. If you do any kind of public speaking, you know that when you get in front of a group of people, you don't just start talking. First you ask for their attention and then wait until the room settles down. You will find it is more effective to report what your needs are: for example, "I need silence, please." You may have to say it more than once. In a one-to-one situation you may say something like this: "I'd like to talk to you about something personal and I want your full attention. When would be a good time?"

Let's think of a couple of effective things you might say to a class, or to your children, or to your partner that would guarantee you'll get their undivided attention. That means reporting your needs instead of asking for something that could get a yes-or-no response. Here are some examples from conversations I've had when I train people to use this technique:

Ann: I feel like when I talk to my husband he's only listening ten percent of the time. I'll just start talking and then notice that he's not really listening and then get annoyed with him.

Diáne: So what might be a better way to get his attention?

Ann: "I have something important I want to tell you. Is now a good time to talk to you, or would there be a better time?"

Diáne: Good. Remember, you're not asking for his attention. You're reporting what you want from them, and that is what you did. He will need to respond with a time instead of a yes or no. It would be even more effective if your second sentence was, "What time would work for you?"

Jonathan: "I need to talk with you for a while about certain things. Would this be a good time for you?"

Diáne: In the first part of your statement you told him/her what you wanted, which is good. And then you asked the question about a good time in a manner that allows a yes-or-no answer. It would have been stronger to say, "What would be a good time?" In your scenario though, they might say "no." Then you could still say, "Okay, let's decide on a time that would be good for both of us."

Maria: I'm more direct. Usually with my husband I'll look to get eye contact and then say, "Sweetie, I have something important to say. Is now a good time?"

Diáne: That is pretty direct, but he can still say no. It might work better to say, "I would love to talk now, if that works for you," because then he becomes engaged in the negotiation.

Imagine the relationship as a canoe with each person sitting on opposite sides. If only one person is paddling (expressing their needs), that boat is going to tip or spin in circles. To have good communication, both people must share and bring their needs into the center of the boat. That will keep the balance.

There is a simple formula that integrates timing and language:

- *Say what you really want using an "I" statement, a statement about what you want or need.* "I'd really love some flowers tonight." "I'd like to go out to a restaurant for dinner." "I would like the garbage taken out." "I'd like to be shown where the produce is in this supermarket."

- *Then say how it will affect you if you get what you want or need.* "It would make me really happy if you did it now" or "I'd appreciate that very much." Most people want to please others—they want to know how to do that.

This also works if you're angry. Let's say someone is always late or they've broken a rule and you're angry about it. "I'm really feeling angry and disappointed right now" works better than "Why do you always have to come late?" "I'm so disappointed that our agreement didn't hold" works better than "Why don't you do what you say you're going to do"?

The reason you focus on yourself, on your "I statement," is that you don't want to put the other person in a defensive position. So make it all about you and your feelings and keep the focus on the situation, not on the other person. You're not going for "I really feel pissed off because you came in late" or "I really feel pissed off because you didn't pay me back the money." Instead, it's "I really feel hurt because the agreement we made about my being paid back the money has not been honored." There's no accusing language in that.

How do you think you would feel if you came in late to a meeting and someone said to you, "This is the third time you've come in late. I'm really sick of it." How do your feelings shift if instead you hear "I'm really annoyed that the time frame for our meetings is not being kept."

The power in power language is in saying what you mean, using the right words—effective, true words in "I" statements. Even if you don't get what you want, the formula of using "I" statements opens the door to further dialogue, rather than to just a yes-or-no answer or defensiveness. It also means you have expressed yourself authentically regardless of outcome. In essence, you're creating a container for the other person to step into, a place of truth and assertiveness. If they can meet you there in the same way, then you can talk or negotiate. If you say, "I really want to go to the movies tonight and I'd love it if you'd come with me" and the answer is "I'm really tired. I don't want to go to the movies tonight," it's not about you. The other person will probably add something like "but maybe we can go another time." Do you see how much more open this conversation is than if you simply ask, "Will you go to the movies with me?" The answer to that question can only be yes or no, and there's no space for a real dialogue there.

My students and clients become more empowered when they practice power language. It's honoring yourself. How many people come to sound healers because they lack confidence or they feel small? So many people dishonor themselves. They don't even know they're doing it and they don't know how to reverse it. They have bad relationships over and over again. People have stepped on them, dishonored them, involved them in alcoholic relationships or relationships with power plays. Power language is more about honoring yourself than the result it's going to get you. The surprise is that it will get you the result you want much more often than if you communicate without this awareness.

Silence Is Golden

I used to raise funds for the Chamber of Commerce, and I learned how to ask businesses for grants for events. I'd say, "What we'd like is a contribution of ten thousand dollars"—and then I'd be silent. When you act powerfully but are uncomfortable with the silence that follows, it's tempting take it back: "I'd like a contribution of ten thousand dollars. But if you don't have it, it will be okay." Or how about this one: "I'd really love it if you drove me to the airport at four o'clock in the morning … but I know it's early and if you can't do it, it's okay. I'll find another way." The key is to say what you have to say, say how it'll affect you if you get it, and then quietly wait for a response.

Now you have seen the power of using the right words at the right time in the right way. This will only help you if you practice until the techniques are second nature. Practice avoiding *asking* for something. Instead use the formula: say what you want using "I" statements. Say how it will affect you if you get it. Then be silent and wait for a response.

You might consider going to the grocery store just to practice the formula in a nonthreatening situation. Instead of saying, "Can you tell me where the soap is?" say, "I need some soap. I'd like it if you'd take me to the right aisle."

Creating Boundaries

Another important area that will help you communicate with family, friends, practice partners, and clients is the ability to create boundaries. And that means being able to say no.

Saying no can be unpleasant because it can bring up feelings of guilt, weakness, or selfishness. But if you don't maintain boundaries and instead do things out of a sense of obligation, you can become resentful. Being able to create boundaries and honor your truth is vital to being in integrity with yourself.

Know that boundaries are a way of honoring yourself, acknowledging that you are as important as anyone else. With boundaries, you are in a position to say yes when you mean yes, no when you mean no, and I don't know when you have not made a decision or are unsure.

Instead of using the word no, say something like "That doesn't work for me." If your answer is ultimately no, you can leave it at that. If it's no—but just for now, you can add, "What would work better for me is …" Here's an example:

> Q: Will you make two hundred cookies for the Brownie meeting tomorrow?
>
> A: Oh, I am so sorry, but that doesn't work for me for tomorrow. Or,
>
> A: Oh, I am sorry, but that doesn't work for me. I could make fifty though. Or,
>
> A: Oh, I am sorry, but that doesn't work for me. I could make them next time with a week's advance notice.

These are ways of saying no in a softer way, and if you want to you can still add your terms to it to make it into a yes. Notice I didn't add a lot of explanation or attempt to justify my answer. Think of how you might normally respond to a request when you don't want to do what's being asked of you, and try one of these methods instead. Always keep the tone friendly and neutral.

People are so happy to comply when you say how you feel about the situation. After you have practiced for a while, you'll think, *Oh, my God. Why haven't I always done this?* I shared this method with a single dad whose kids weren't doing what he asked a lot of the time. The next time I saw him, he said, "I'm doing this with all my employees now. This is so easy! It's so easy to get people to do what I want them to do, and to get what I want more of the time."

Practice power language a little at a time until it feels second nature to you. You will find that communicating more effectively is very empowering.

Closing Thoughts

When I first began to explore sound healing with the bowls and other instruments, there was no introductory "operating manual" describing how to do it. With this book, I have aimed to fill that void, sharing much of the knowledge I have gained over decades of hands-on healing work and thousands of hours of practice. It is my hope and wish that you will find this book a trusty guide and companion as you embark on your own sound healing practice. May you enjoy the beautiful, healing world of the sacred instruments!

Acknowledgments

Many thanks to all the good people over the years who have helped me expand my knowledge base and experience—which turned into this book.

To my children, Isaiah and Stefan, for keeping me real and giving me many opportunities to practice unconditional love.

To my life partner, Richard, for his unending support of whatever I have wanted to do—and for being my first Tibetan bowl teacher.

To my friends Susan Murray and Joan Thatcher for reading and correcting many initial manuscripts.

To all my students for helping me refine how I do what I do to make it more accessible, and for all your questions and questioning.

To my wonderful editor, Sheridan McCarthy, for practicing skillful means to mentor me through combining my work into this book.

To Cheryl di Ciantis for the multiple edits and resending of her wonderful illustrations.

To my publisher, Teri Rider for her patience, guidance and aplomb at working through the challenges of publishing this book.

Appendix A
Sound Healing Pioneers

Sound has the power to heal our wounds, ignite our spirit, change consciousness, and re-unite us with the divine harmonies and rhythms of the universe. Through this unified vision and increased ability to hear the sounds of the cosmos within ourselves we access health and wholeness.

Donna Carey, founder, Kairos Institute of Healing

In recent years sound healing has rapidly gained recognition as an effective healing modality. It has been shown to be an integral part of the healing process for cancer patients. It is also effective in relieving pain, in reducing stress, and in the treatment of stress-related afflictions such as fibromyalgia, tumors, insomnia, chronic fatigue syndrome, depression, nervous disorders, and more.

For at least twenty years a number of mainstream medical doctors, scientists, and holistic practitioners have worked with different varieties of sound, and their findings have been well documented. Some of them include:

Dr. Mitchell Gaynor

The late Dr. Gaynor was director of medical oncology and integrative medicine at the Strang Cancer Prevention Center Institute in New York. For about eight years he used sound, including Tibetan bowls, crystal bowls, and chanting, in work with cancer patients, achieving enormous success.

In his excellent book *The Healing Power of Sound*, Gaynor writes:

> If we accept that sound is vibration, and we know that vibration touches every part of our physical being, then we understand that sound is "heard" not only through our ears but through every cell in our body.... One reason sound

heals on a physical level is because it so deeply touches and transforms us on the emotional and spiritual planes. Sound can redress imbalances on every level of physiologic functioning and can play a positive role in the treatment of virtually any medical disorder.[9]

Dr. Gaynor's research showed that the sound vibration of the bowls affects the disrhythmic motion found in cancer cells, causing a harmonious transformation. In a blind study he found a 50 percent shorter recovery time for chemo patients who used the bowls regularly. He also discovered that when bowls were used in the early stages of cancer during consultations with patients, their anxiety and stress were greatly reduced.

Imagine how much the decision making about a patient's future would improve in an atmosphere devoid of stress and anxiety. Imagine also how the ability to repeatedly connect with that sense of tranquility during the discomfort of chemotherapy would increase the quality of life for these patients. It simply makes sense.

Dr. David Simon

Dr. Simon was medical director of neurological services at Sharp Cabrillo Hospital in San Diego and director of medical services at the renowned Chopra Center in Carlsbad, California. In his work he found that specific chants are chemically metabolized into what he termed "endogenous opiates" that act on the body as internal painkillers and healing agents.

Sara Lazar

In 2008 the journal *Alternative Therapies in Health and Medicine* published a review of twenty studies of brain-wave entrainment and patient outcomes. The conclusion was that brain-wave entrainment is an effective tool to use on cognitive functioning deficits, stress, pain, headaches, and premenstrual syndrome. The studies also suggest that sound work can help with behavioral problems.[10] Brain-wave entrainment is one of the principal characteristics of healing with the sacred sound instruments.

Fabien Maman

Fabien Maman took the dramatic and fascinating photographs of cotton cells shown in Chapter 1. He has taken many other photos of cells, including cancer cells, as they are impacted by sound. Take a moment to visit his website and look at his photos at http://tama-do.com. This visual evidence of the impact of sound on physiology is striking.

Dr. Jeffery Thompson

Founder of the Center for Neuroacoustic Research in Carlsbad, California, and formerly a chiropractor, Thompson focuses on helping clients find their fundamental sound frequency, the brain-wave patterns associated with their optimal health, by using a special table that is designed to send sound vibrations through the body.

Wayne Perry and Jonathan Goldman

Wayne Perry, author of *Sound Medicine*,[11] and Jonathan Goldman, director of the Sound Healers Association and author of *Healing Sounds*,[12] have spent years working with the sound of the human voice (toning), overtone chanting, and the positive effects they have on healing.

Richard Rudis

Richard Rudis (Karma Sonam Dorje) is internationally known as a sacred sound educator. He co-conducts advanced workshops at my Tibetan Bowl Sound Healing School, teaches the Buddhist dharma through the Himalayan instruments, and conducts harmonic gong baths. He has been recognized nationally as a featured gong master by Paiste gongs (paistegongs.com) and has appeared in the documentary film *Stupa* by William Schaffer. Numerous cases of spontaneous healings have taken place at his events.

My Own Work: Observing the Effects

I have conducted my own research with sound using biofeedback equipment and have found that the high-frequency harmonics that the singing bowls produce have transformative abilities—impacting brain activity, heart rate, and body temperature—facilitating a deeply peaceful state of being while also energizing the brain.

A Recent Study

In 2016, I was invited to Portland, Oregon, to conduct a noncontrolled study of singing bowl therapy at the National University of Natural Medicine with researcher Nikolajs Beikoff- Strands. For this research project, I worked with fourteen clients doing single sessions with each.

Among the findings from the study were these:

- Participants experienced a significant decrease in mean heart rate following a session, indicating that singing bowl therapy may enhance parasympathetic nervous system activation, thus having a relaxing effect on the autonomic nervous system.
- These nervous system changes suggest that people with a high level of stress, anxiety, or attention deficit may receive particular benefit from singing bowl therapy.
- In follow-up questionnaire responses, participants reported experiencing enhanced attention to and awareness of the present moment.
- They also reported experiencing enhanced positive feelings of aliveness and alertness, and of having energy available to the self.
- Participants' responses and comments hint at a deeper meaning than the data collected show. There seem to be audible, physical, and energetic features created through the playing of singing bowls with intention.

I have received countless comments from clients over the years attesting to the healing effects of a session with the sacred sound instruments, and it does not surprise me that researchers have been able to quantify some of these impacts. It is my hope that further study will continue to deepen our understanding from a scientific point of view.

APPENDIX B
A Case Study in Hidden Belief Systems

Following is an example of recognizing the larger symbolism (hidden belief systems) within issues that are presented to us as sound healers and making associations with out-of-balance elements:

The clients are a father and son. The father's issues are deep, recurrent patterns of depression that he associates with childhood abuse, both sexual and frequent beatings. Having explored many different paths to change his patterns, he still feels stuck.

The son presents with issues of having a very short fuse (frequent anger), poor relationships because of that anger, bouts of depression, and a longing for a sense of flow.

What's the underlining message both of them hold? "I'm worthless, I am crap, I am damaged goods." This message is passed on from and between the father and son, manifesting in a multitude of behaviors.

So anger and depression are present. Anger is fire energy. Depression is Earth energy. Where is fire situated in the body? Where is it happening and where is it going? The home base of fire energy is the solar plexus, the center of will, self-esteem, and self-honor. (Refer to the diagram and the elemental long lines.)

Keeping in mind that all things are interrelated, there are many points at play here. Abuse and anger issues related to trust, self-esteem, fear, the ability to love, control—all these things are touched. Anger and depression rooted in the Fire and Earth elements are perhaps

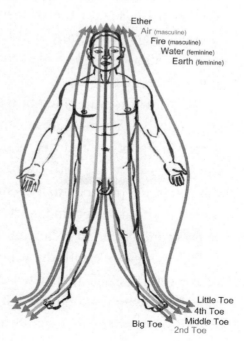

Ether
Air (masculine)
Fire (masculine)
Water (feminine)
Earth (feminine)

Little Toe
4th Toe
Middle Toe
2nd Toe
Big Toe

central, but so are water (flow of life, receptivity, relationships), air (the ability to think clearly), and ether (a sense of expansiveness in life).

I told these clients this story about the diamond: The diamond is a gem that retains its inherent qualities, no matter what happens to it. If you smash a diamond, the little pieces of diamond are still diamonds, and if you take a diamond and bury it under mountains of refuse, when it's retrieved it's still a diamond, no matter how much garbage is on or around it. It still maintains its inherent qualities. Our work together was to reconnect with the diamond within themselves and begin to see how their life's trauma could provide them with a doorway to greater compassion and resilience. Finding a way to embrace the unacceptable is where the healing begins.

Now to questions from students, and further into the case study to illustrate the answers:

How do we work with Fire energy, in terms of releasing and redirecting it? What kind of energy might you want to balance it with elementally?

As always, you have a variety of options. One is to balance the Fire and Earth lines with the tridoshas and conduct all the bowl work in a downward and/or clockwise direction to ground and dissipate the anger. It would also be a good idea to break up the stagnation in the root by gently clacking the ganta.

We know the water long line is associated with the heart and the sacral area, and the sacrum stores deep sadness, grief, and trauma. The son has anger (fire energy) and depression (stuck Earth). Earth energy can take a long time to work with—it can feel like slow-moving sludge or clay. It represents deeply rooted, longstanding issues, so patience is needed to penetrate these issues and start moving energy. His life is not flowing, so that's an indication to balance fire with water.

Before we work with the water field, we need to clear it, unblock it. But once we unblock it, then what do we do? This is a perfect time to move water energy up the long line with a ganta, and then do the infinity pattern over the entire body to integrate and create balance with the other elements.

The figure eight is balancing, and creating that pattern in a clockwise direction is expanding its reach, as if his body is a radiator and water energy is moving through it, creating a sense of flow.

After I did this work with the son, he said to me, "I probably relate more to that diamond than you believe."

I replied, "It doesn't matter what I believe. What matters is how you view yourself and how that impacts your choices in life. My sense is that the anger you are feeling is the recognition of your worthiness, of your diamond self, but that recognition does not know how to manifest. It doesn't know how to get through the obstacles that block it."

At this point, the boy, who was seventeen, began to cry, saying, "You just hit a nerve."

That's the release. When that happened, he was in a very relaxed state, the tears began to flow, and he just needed encouragement to allow the emotions to come out. Then I did the most soothing work I could with all the instruments, knowing that now he was open to remembering the feeling of alignment. When we finished, he just lay there with his eyes open, feeling who he knew he was. He couldn't speak.

Could he hold that feeling for a long time? That will be challenging. Habitual patterns need time and repetition to shift, so a series of sessions is important. But the most important thing is that he touched his essence for the first time. He was able to touch who he really was.

Appendix C
Testimonials and Stories

Testimonials

Over the years I have received numerous letters, emails, and conversations about people's experiences with the bowls: clients, other sound healing practitioners, and students. The comments that follow are just a few of the vast number of communications I have received. For confidentiality's sake, I have omitted the names.

> *"Oh my God!!! I've been holding way too much stuff that isn't mine, with covered up anger and embarrassment and with an inner excuse that I can't get away from it because I'm sick … and yet it is this whole thing that has made me sick, with my unconscious permission …*
>
> I'm now working at loving myself better, and releasing and putting things in the right perspective. I read a book about self-healing long ago and got good insight then, but I'm a different person now and this really is a different view. Wow, what a trip … I don't have to do this stuff anymore and I have the power to free myself, even though others don't behave right, and it doesn't seem like it on the surface in regards to my circumstances. I am already beginning to feel some inner lifting and relief happening in my heart chakra and solar plexus. This bowl therapy is really opening me up and helping me to see things better. Thanks."
>
> "Yesterday I was walking with my dog and she was attacked by some neighbor dogs. They didn't break skin; I think it was just a warning that she was in their territory. She came into the house and was clearly a little traumatized. I

gave her some Rescue Remedy, which she drank up, and then brushed her to make sure there were no wounds. She still wasn't perking up. Then I played the singing bowl for her. I started out with the lower tones. After striking a particular higher tone she looked up and stared at the bowl. After a while she went into a deeper state of relaxation, breathed deeply (she'd been panting), and stretched out on her back. After my little 'concert' she was able to go back outside."

"I felt a profound sense of peace and vividness that I have never experienced before upon hearing the concert. I could envision colors, sights, and sounds that could only be described as blissful. My only regret is that you are not nearby, as I was deeply moved by the experience."

"I attended your wonderful concert and just wanted to let you know how much I enjoyed it. I am dealing with ovarian cancer (finished chemo in Feb.) and during the concert I felt some interesting sensations in the abdomen. Of course, I was hoping that great healing was taking place. Thanks so much and please come back when you can."

"I had quite a healing that night and it keeps going on and on. I bought your *Tibetan Bowl Sound Healing* CD too. My hip and lower back were in great pain. I couldn't lie flat, knees were up, bottom of feet grew very hot-fire ... then pain melted away from hips, back, feet, neck, shoulder—no pain at all. Then saw myself moving up mountain at evening dusk. Then snow, beautiful. Noticed my head, it seemed to be wide open like in layers. I had to feel my hair to be sure I was okay. Last evening, heard only two pieces and the head opened up again and I saw a person materialize at my feet in golden, orange robe and a bowl-shaped hat on his head walk around me and disappear behind my head. Most interesting. I do not know what to make of all this but I am very interested to know more."

"I am a board-certified osteopathic physician with a practice in this city.... The subtle harmonic tones and overtones of the Tibetan singing bowls created a beautiful and powerful energy that softly enveloped my entire being. I felt any inner stress and anxiety completely disappear as I relaxed into a profound sense of inner calm, peace, and oneness, which I know to be the essential core of my living as a human being, and a true experience of deep inner healing. From this experience, I am convinced that the Tibetan singing bows are an essential part of sound healing and an extremely valuable tool in integrative medicine today, especially for the healing of stress and for pain relief."

Stories

Here are a few notable stories I recall from my sound healing practice. There are many, many more, but these few stand out as I write.

A client who underwent surgery for cancer attributed her sense of peace and the positive outcome of the procedure to playing my CD before, during, and after the surgery.

After two treatments a client recovering from cancer reported that two cysts that that had appeared on her head had liquefied.

An elderly gentleman who was seated on a chair during one of my presentations came up afterward to tell me that his back pain, which had been acute, was completely gone.

A client with a cyst on her ovary reported it gone when she went in for examination after four sessions.

A bird crashed into a window of my house and was stunned. I placed the motionless bird into a box and then played a bowl. Each time I played it around its body and above its head, it closed its eyes. When I stopped playing, it opened them. After five minutes of this, I covered the bird loosely. When I returned a half our later it was gone.

APPENDIX D
Tingsha Chart

Use this chart for tingsha diagnosis. Remember to hold one tingsha close to the body and keep it at a consistent distance as you scan. Do not raise and lower that tingsha to strike it, rather, bring the other tingsha down to it to strike. This way the sound will be consistent. If you think you hear something change in the sound, trust that you do! Create symbols for the following and mark your chart after you scan each section.

Suggested symbols

Tonal Fluttering:

Discordant Tone:

Dropping, swallowing:

Balanced:

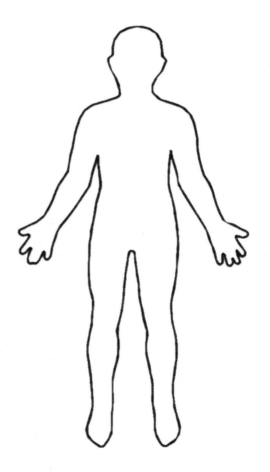

Appendix E

Chart—Stress Effects on Brain and Body

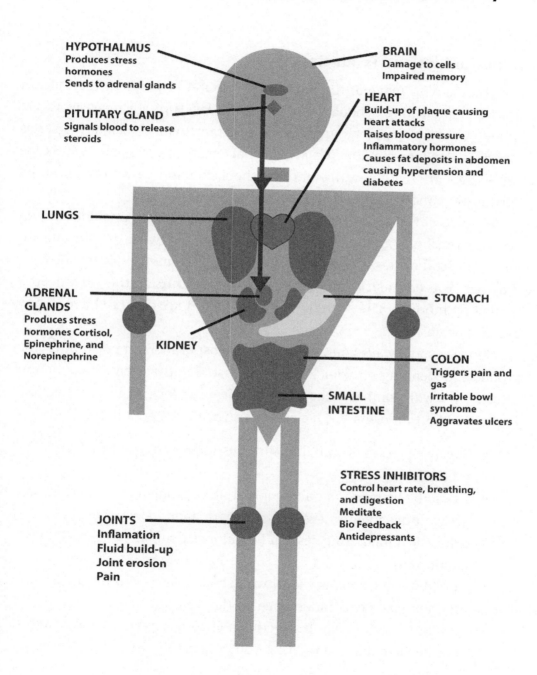

HYPOTHALMUS
Produces stress hormones
Sends to adrenal glands

PITUITARY GLAND
Signals blood to release steroids

BRAIN
Damage to cells
Impaired memory

HEART
Build-up of plaque causing heart attacks
Raises blood pressure
Inflammatory hormones
Causes fat deposits in abdomen causing hypertension and diabetes

LUNGS

ADRENAL GLANDS
Produces stress hormones Cortisol, Epinephrine, and Norepinephrine

KIDNEY

STOMACH

COLON
Triggers pain and gas
Irritable bowl syndrome
Aggravates ulcers

SMALL INTESTINE

STRESS INHIBITORS
Control heart rate, breathing, and digestion
Meditate
Bio Feedback
Antidepressants

JOINTS
Inflamation
Fluid build-up
Joint erosion
Pain

Appendix F
Further Resources

Opportunities and Products

Are you ready to move to the next level of sound healing? At the Tibetan Bowl Sound Healing School, we offer several levels of advanced work via either live workshops or our distance program, which includes a series of videos, student handouts, and personal mentoring sessions via Skype and in person. Visit www.tibetanbowlschool.com and click through to the Certification and Registration pages.

We also carry a complete selection of high-quality ancient singing bowls, tingshas, gantas, dorjes, and gongs as well as Himalayan quartz crystal dorjes, pendulums, and sacred geometric pieces for your practice. You can learn more about the pendulums in the Advanced 3 workshop module. The sacred geometric pieces are good to have in any healing room.

Here are some ways you can make the most of these opportunities and products, depending on your level of interest. See the events page on our website, www.tibetanbowlschool, or call or write for further information: 760-944-3441 (California PST), soundenergyhealing@gmail.com.

- Receive a series of sound healing sessions with a certified professional.
- Ask to be included in our Google student group to exchange ideas, get your questions answered, and learn about teleclasses.
- Schedule a mentoring session (email me at soundenergyhealing@ gmail.com).
- Attend our introductory-level workshop or begin our distance program (see Registration page on the website).
- Call for personal help in selecting a few high-quality bowls, gantas, and tingshas that are right for you, and practice, practice, practice.

- Attend or schedule one of my group or house concerts (see the Events page on the website). I am also available for keynote presentations and lecture demonstrations.
- Take my free online class, "Tibetan Bowls—What You Need to Know," at www.Learnitlive.com. Try this link:https://www. learnitlive.com/view.php?esession_id = 4986&provider_table = cus2_ rec or enter "Diáne Mandle" in the search bar and my classes will come up. Look for the free one.
- Sign up for Diáne's monthly newsletter: http://www. soundenergyhealing.com/pages/contact.html

Notes

Chapter 1

1. Jeanne Achterberg, *Imagery in Healing: Shamanism and Modern Medicine* (Boston: Shambhala, 1985), 19.
2. Personal conversation with Richard Rudis.
3. Personal conversation with Richard Rudis.
4. *The Tao of Sound: Acoustic Sound Healing for the 21st Century* (Tama-Do, The Academy of Sound, Color and Movement), 2008.
5. Masaru Emoto, *The Hidden Messages in Water* (New York: Atria Books), 2005.

Chapter 2 through Appendix A

1. Ibid, 85–6.
2. Richard Rudis, Ezinearticles.com, "July Fifteenth; Tibetan Plateau," http://ezinearticles.com/?July-Fifteenth;-Tibetan-Plateau&id = 242894.
3. From a recorded teleclass.
4. American Polarity Therapy Association, "What Is Polarity?," http://www.polaritytherapy.org/polarity-therapy/.
5. Jonathan Goldman, *Healing Sounds: The Power of Harmonics* (Rochester, VT: Healing Arts/Inner Tradition), 1992.
6. Linda Carroll, "Personality May Be Set by Preschool," NBC News, Children's Health, http://www.nbcnews.com/id/22554554/ns/health-childrens_health/t/personality-may-be-set-preschool/#.WPaWjxHHeM8.
7. Jennifer Hunter, "Don't Believe Everything You Think," Cleveland Clinic Wellness, http://www.clevelandclinicwellness.com/DailyDose/archive/2014/08/12/Dont-Believe-Everything-You-Think.aspx.
8. Angeles Arrien, *The Four-Fold Way: Walking the Paths of the Warrior, Teacher, Healer and Visionary* (New York: HarperOne) 1993.
9. Mitchell L. Gaynor, *The Healing Power of Sound: Recovery from Life-Threatening Illness Using Sound, Voice, and Music* (Boston: Shambhala, 1999), 17.
10. Kathryn Drury Wagner, "The Science Behind Healing with Sound," http://spiritualityhealth.com/articles/science-behind-healing-sound.
11. Wayne Perry, Sound Medicine, (Musikarma Publishing, 2007). CreateSpace, 2012.
12. Jonathan Goldman, Healing Sounds: *The Power of Harmonics* (Rochester, VT: Healing Arts Press, 2002).

Bibliography and Recordings

Diáne Mandle, *The Book of Hard Knocks* (just kidding)

Diáne Mandle, *How to Clear Space with Sound Using Tibetan Bowls and Tingshas*, Aardvark Publishing, 2007

Angeles Arrien, *The Four-Fold Way*, HarperSanFrancisco, 1983

Joachim Ernst Berendt, *The World Is Sound: Music and the Landscape of Consciousness*, Destiny Books, 1991

Hans Cousto, *The Cosmic Octave*, LifeRhythm, 1988

Lama Surya Das, *Awakening the Buddha Within*, Broadway Books, 1997

Mitchell L. Gaynor, *The Healing Power of Sound*, Shambhala Publications, 1999

Jonathan Goldman, *Healing Sounds: The Power of Harmonics*, Healing Arts, 1992

Louise Hay, *You Can Heal Your Life*, Hay House, 1984

Anneke Huyser, *Singing Bowl Exercises for Personal Harmony*, Binkey Kok Publications, 1999

Eva Rudy Jansen, *Singing Bowls: A Practical Handbook of Instruction and Use*, Binkey Kok Publications, 1992

Laurel Elizabeth Keys, *Toning: The Creative Power of the Voice*, DeVorss, 1973

Robert Lawlor, *Sacred Geometry: Philosophy and Practice*, Thames & Hudson, 1982

Nancy Anna Risley, *The Polarity Workbook*, Polarity Realization Institute, 1990

Pierre Sollier, *Listening for Wellness*, Mozart Center Press, 2005

CDs/MP3s:

Diáne Mandle:
  Tibetan Bowl Sound Healing (Tibetan bowls)
  Sarasvati's Dream (bowls, gongs, didgeridoo, and percussion)
  Being Well: The Journey (three guided meditations enveloped in the sound of bowls, gong, and more)

Richard Rudis (Karma Sonam Dorje) Planetary Earth Gong CDs:
  Terma-Yana
  Event Horizon
    Pilgrim's Prayer
    Tibetan Pilgrimage

About the Author

Diáne Mandle is an internationally known sound healer, teacher, Sounds True recording artist, and author based in San Diego. A frequent presenter at the Deepak Chopra Center, the Golden Door, and Rancho la Puerta, she has been part of the Integrative Therapy Team at San Diego Cancer Center, presents workshops for cancer patients at Sharp and Scripps hospitals, and has developed and conducted a program for incarcerated veterans with PTSD. Diáne offers workshops and concerts internationally and operates the Tibetan Bowl Sound Healing School in Southern California. She is featured along with healers such as Deepak Chopra and John Gray in the video series *Tao—Living in Balance*.

In her present life and as a former regional director of the American Cancer Society, Chamber of Commerce director, and transformational coach, Diáne's objective has always been to bring hope and well-being by helping people develop empowering belief systems and perspectives, and deeper insights into their personal and professional lives.

Being French-American has gifted Diáne with the ability to live and travel worldwide, often using the arts as a means of connecting with people in multicultural contexts. She brings her rich background to her work and life in service to all. Diáne now lives in Southern California, where in addition to her sound healing practice, she loves to paint, perform in theater, and ride her bike!

Printed in Great Britain
by Amazon

29126437R00150